Called to High Adventure:

A Fresh Look at the Holy Spirit and the Spirit-Filled Life

By Dr. Clayton Ford

Spiritual Journey Press
P.O. Box 3041
Mercerville, NJ 08619
www.spiritualjourneypress.com

Called to High Adventure:
A Fresh Look at the Holy Spirit and the Spirit-Filled Life

ISBN: 0-9709666-6-0
ISBN 13: 978-0-9709666-6-7
Library of Congress Control Number: 2010924805

A Spiritual Journey Press Book: Second Printing 2011

Queries regarding rights and permissions should be addressed to Spiritual Journey Press, P.O. Box 3041, Mercerville, NJ 08619. For e-mail communication, write to the author at claytonford@sbcglobal.net or SJourneyPress@comcast.net. Please write for bulk purchase, church and study group discounts.

Printed in the United States by Morris Publishing®
3212 East Highway 30
Kearney, NE 68847
1-800-650-7888

DEDICATION

I dedicate this book to my amazing Christian mother, Virginia M. Ford, who at the time of this writing is ninety years of age. Her faithful witness and her daily prayers for my spiritual and general well-being are more responsible for my salvation than any other factor, excepting the wondrous grace of Jesus. Words do not suffice in trying to describe how much she means to me, and to all of her family and friends.

ACKNOWLEDGMENTS

My wife Cheri has spent many hours helping me with this book. She is an author in her own right, having published five books herself (cherylford.com). Thank you, Cheri!

My mother Virginia Ford is no doubt my biggest fan and chief intercessor. She has prayed fervently for the writing and publishing of this book, and I am enormously grateful for her.

The prayer support and encouragement of our two children have been a great blessing. Billy (with wife Denise and their five kids) is a Baptist pastor (bouquetcanyonchurch.com) and Hannah is a worship leader and Christian singer/songwriter (hannahford.com) with three CDs to her credit.

I thank my fellow leaders of Holy Spirit Renewal Ministries (hsrm.org) whose prayers and partnership in fostering Holy Spirit renewal around the country have been wonderful. I also express my deep appreciation to Klein and Karen Gilhousen for their support.

Thanks also to the members of La Jolla Christian Fellowship (lajollacf.org) for their prayers and for their encouragement of my renewal ministry that extends beyond our church. The measure of God's grace that we are experiencing in ministry together is nothing short of miraculous.

I also want to thank Dr. Lee Spitzer, Executive Minister and Senior Regional Pastor of the ABC of New Jersey, who is the editor and publisher of this book. I deeply appreciate his willingness to work with me on this project.

Finally, and most importantly, I thank God, without whom my life would have no core nor compass, but with whom life is a never-ending adventure. I love Him and am genuinely grateful for His faithfulness and generosity toward me.

Dr. Clay Ford
March 10, 2010

Called to High Adventure:
A Fresh Look at the Holy Spirit and the Spirit-Filled Life

Contents

INTRODUCTION

Scene One

Some years ago, as I walked through the parking lot of my church, a young woman I did not know approached me. She explained that she attended another local congregation and was looking for someone from our church to ask questions about one of our programs. In the course of our conversation, she happened to mention that her husband was a Spirit-filled Christian and that she was not. Because I'd been involved for some years in the Holy Spirit renewal movement, the term "Spirit-filled" was a familiar one. The interpretation was simple enough to me: Obviously, she meant her husband had experienced a powerful filling of the Holy Spirit that released him in a new way to honor and glorify Jesus Christ.

As we continued our talk, she opened up and shared some deep hurts in her life. She described how her husband abused alcohol and frequently went out with other women. On the other hand, she remained faithful to both him and God. She actively served her church in various ways, including Sunday School teaching. As she described her great love and devotion for Christ, I saw her eyes glisten. Tears fell as she shared the heartbreak of living with a drunken and adulterous man. Since she appeared to be a lovely, Spirit-filled Christian, I felt perplexed. "OK, I've got to straighten this out," I told myself.

"I think I misunderstood you," I said. "I thought I heard you say that your *husband* is Spirit-filled but *you* are not. You must have meant that *you* are Spirit-filled while your *husband* is not."

"No," she answered, "You understood right. My husband *is* Spirit-filled."

Baffled, I asked, "Well, how can your husband be filled with the Spirit if he's a drunken adulterer?"

She replied, "Well, he speaks in tongues . . . and I don't."

Scene Two

I had heard of a coffeehouse ministry from a young adult in the Baptist church where I served. "The Holy Spirit is really moving there," he said. God's Spirit had recently touched me in a deeper way, and I was eager to learn more. So one night I stole over to see what God was up to at this coffeehouse. The mood was happy, and I enjoyed the music and singing. Then suddenly, right when I was feeling pretty much at home, everyone jumped to their feet and began screaming and shouting at the top of their lungs. They stomped the floor, flailed their arms, turned in circles, all the while screaming. There I was, confused and frightened, wondering what might come next. Rather than sticking around to find out, I beat a hasty retreat, vowing never to return.

Scene Three

Our women had enjoyed a *great* women's retreat. They came home all aglow and overjoyed. Many had experienced a filling of the Holy Spirit, and quite a number now claimed to have the gift of speaking in tongues. As the church's pastor, hearing the wonderful things God had done excited me. While I was basically receptive to tongues and the other spiritual gifts mentioned in the New Testament, I did expect biblical balance concerning these things in our church.

The women were so excited that they asked me if we could have the retreat speaker and her husband come minister to our entire fellowship on a Wednesday night. I said that would be fine, and we made the arrangements. The meeting was well attended. Most of the women who had attended the retreat came, excitedly expecting the spiritual blessings to spread. Many more of our number came, too—some eager, some curious, and others cautious. The husband and wife team shared many exciting stories and testimonies of God moving in miraculous ways by the Spirit's power. We all felt hungry to see these things happen in our midst.

The woman shifted her message to teach specifically about the Holy Spirit. She stressed repeatedly the necessity of receiving "the baptism in the Holy Spirit" and of speaking in tongues as the evidence of that experience. I had heard this before, but even I was unprepared for what came next. "Do you know that the Bible *commands* you to speak in tongues?" she asked.

Our silence told her that we didn't know this. So she said, "Turn in your Bibles to Ephesians 6:18. See, it says there that we're supposed to pray at all times in the Spirit. That's God's command for *everyone* to speak in tongues."

Scene Four

My wife Cheri and I stayed as guests in a lovely apartment on the grounds of a Northern California mission organization. I had been asked to do four days of teaching at their training school. Seventeen students attended my class, ranging in age from eighteen to fifty-something. While the group represented a variety of church backgrounds and spiritual experiences, most came from Pentecostal and charismatic churches.

My assigned topic that week was "The Person and Working of the Holy Spirit." Before I began my series of teachings, I thought I'd get to know the students a bit. I asked each to share his or her experience and understanding of the Holy Spirit and to be honest about such things as the following: "Are you confused about the work of the Holy Spirit? Do you speak in tongues? If not, have you felt pressured about it? Has someone ever made you feel inferior or second class in matters of the Holy Spirit?"

This time of open sharing proved shocking to the students. At least half said they felt confused about such things as "the baptism of the Spirit," "speaking in tongues," and being "Spirit-filled." Nearly half had felt pressured and made to feel inferior when their spiritual experiences didn't follow the pattern expected in their churches. Thinking, "I'm the only one in the group who feels this way," they had hidden their feelings. What a revelation they had when they heard so many other fellow students sharing a similar confusing struggle!

Scene Five

Cheri and I sat in the right front section of a large auditorium. Our section of seats sat off to the side and at an angle. This way we enjoyed a good view, not only of the platform area, but also of the front and far side of the first row. A thousand or more believers from all over the world had crowded together for this typical Saturday night renewal meeting.

The front row seemed filled primarily with leaders, counselors, and those authorized as prayer ministers. The praise team opened the service, leading praise songs to God. As the service progressed, I noticed an increasing number of those in the front row bobbing and jerking. Worship ended and people took their seats in excited anticipation of the message. By then, it seemed that perhaps two thirds or more of the front row (thirty or forty people) were bobbing and jerking uncontrollably. Obviously, they enjoyed this, and no one seemed to think their behavior out of the ordinary. Gazing at this incredible scene, I found myself wondering, "God, I'm finally feeling some hope for unity over the issue of tongues . . . and now THIS?!"

Experiences like the preceding scenarios highlight some of the concerns that led me to write this book. A great deal of confusion exists within Christ's body over issues related to how the Holy Spirit works in individual Christians and churches. Believers hold widely divergent views on the issues raised in the preceding five scenes. Often our differences both in doctrine and in practice create suspicion, division, and even outright hostility within Christ's body.

Over the years, I have read and studied much about the Holy Spirit and His work. Rarely, have I found a book that provides a theological foundation capable of building bridges rather than barricades between Christians. Most authors and teachers either cast their lot with the Pentecostal/charismatic stream of theology or with the fundamentalist/evangelical, non-charismatic stream. Different understandings related to issues like "the baptism in the Holy Spirit," "speaking in tongues," "being filled with the Spirit" are generally so at odds with each other that they often exclude the other's point of view completely.

Some pastors, radio preachers, and authors have gone so far as to say that tongues is of the devil. Others don't go that far but still find a way to denigrate the gift of tongues: One Sunday evening, I visited the church of a nationally known leader and heard him describe a second experience following conversion that involves a breaking of one's will so that Christ can truly be Lord. He shocked me when he added, "But I'm not talking about tongues or any of that kind of foolishness*!*"

On the other hand, Pentecostal and charismatic believers can make statements that create a definite impression that if you don't speak with tongues, you have a defective or sub-standard Christian life. "Do you have the baptism?" (translated, "Do you speak in tongues?") often carries with it the insinuation that tongues is the spiritual litmus test for determining who is and who is not Spirit-filled.

To serve as pastor of at least one particular denomination, the pastoral candidate *must* speak in tongues, whereas in another denomination the requirement is precisely the opposite — the candidate *does not, must not, and will not ever* speak in tongues.

These aren't even the most extreme positions — some make tongues necessary for salvation while others make it a sure ticket to hell! But these present serious differences that can certainly quench the Holy Spirit and hinder if not prevent a deeper unity and cooperation among Christians and Christian communities. Even when wonderful manifestations of Christian solidarity can be found in ministers' groups or in jointly-sponsored events, issues of the Holy Spirit are seldom dealt with, assuring a limited unity at best.

This book does not focus primarily on the issue of speaking in tongues. However, since this gift does tend to cause controversy, we will address it in some depth. Still, this book's purpose goes much deeper. *My purpose is to bring to the theological table, so to speak, a new approach to understanding the work of the Holy Spirit, an approach that God has already been using to build bridges upon which Christians can come together rather than barricades which drive them further apart.*

Is it not grievous that the Holy Spirit, whom God gave to the church for creating true community in Christ, is the One around whom so much controversy and division exist? Doesn't it stand to reason that, *because the Holy Spirit has been given in large measure* to *create, build up, and unite the body of Christ, we ought to be able to teach about Him and His workings in a way that accomplishes His purpose?* We need a balanced biblical understanding of the Holy Spirit's ministry that unites Christ's body; that embraces all He has to give us without creating a "haves-versus-have-nots" division or mentality; that celebrates our unity in Christ and also affirms our diverse spiritual gifts and experiences.

My earnest prayer is that this book will clear up unnecessary confusion and division surrounding the workings of the Holy Spirit and that, by God's grace, it will present a helpful and balanced approach in answer to such questions as "What is the baptism with the Holy Spirit?" "What does it mean to be filled with the Spirit?" "What is speaking in tongues? Is it for today? Is it for everyone?" and so on. My general approach to these questions is different than either the classic-Pentecostal/charismatics or the non-charismatic evangelicals. I can explain this, at least in part, by telling you that I am a longstanding Baptist pastor who has sought to bring balanced Holy Spirit renewal in Baptist churches I have served and in my denomination. As National Chair of Holy Spirit Renewal Ministries (HSRM.org), I have organized and spoken at many renewal conferences on regional and national levels, as well as in numerous churches.

My theological approach to these issues has grown from a deep desire to open the full range of the Holy Spirit's ministry to Bible-believing Christians without creating non-biblical theological divisions. *I believe this approach is more solidly biblical and scripturally balanced than either of the two most commonly held views, and that it has the potential to bring us together in unity so that the Christian church is no longer divided over the ministry of the Holy Spirit.* (For more about the theological approach and the principles of biblical interpretation employed to write this book, see Appendix A: "Rightly Dividing the Word of Truth.")

In addition to the purpose of bringing Christians together in their understanding and experience of the ministry of the Holy Spirit, I have another extremely important reason for writing this book: *WE NEED THE HOLY SPIRIT!* And what's more, we all *know* we need more of the Holy Spirit. In conversations with leaders across the country, I hear it over and over again. Just a few examples:

> *We're out of balance when we talk about the Father and the Son but leave out the Holy Spirit. The Holy Spirit provides life, vitality–that's why it is so important to emphasize His role.*
> (Dr. Charles Revis, Executive Minister of the American Baptist Churches in the Northwest)

> *Misguided theologies and fear of extreme behaviors are reasons why pastors and leaders do not embrace the fullness of the Holy Spirit. But without the moving of the Spirit, in whatever fashion He manifests Himself, I don't believe renewal can take place. Where God's people are open to the fullness of His Spirit, there is excitement, a sense of expectancy; but when a church isn't willing to explore what God might do through the Holy Spirit, you see a stagnation in that church.* (Dr. Larry Swain, Executive Minister, American Baptist Churches of Ohio)

I believe the work of Holy Spirit Renewal Ministries is of the utmost importance to help renew and strengthen the witness of all of our churches and our entire denomination. (Rev. Dr. Alice Greene, National President of the ABCUSA Ministers' Council and Pastor of Irving Park Baptist Church, Chicago)

In light of the fact that all of us know we need more of the Holy Spirit, Chapter 8 provides an opportunity for each of us to pray through important steps to receive and walk in the fullness of the Holy Spirit. Paul the apostle wrote "the kingdom of God is not a matter of talk but of power" (1 Corinthians 4:20). It's not adequate simply to talk (or write) about the ministry of the Holy Spirit. We must also *experience* Him, personally and corporately, and appropriate the power and gifts He makes available for serving Him. To these ends, let us begin.

CHAPTER 1

What Is the Baptism in the Holy Spirit?

What is "the baptism in the Holy Spirit?" Isn't this the crucial question and starting point? Are not our differences in understanding this particular experience or reality at the crux of most of our divisions over the Holy Spirit?

The general position of the Pentecostal/charismatic tradition is that the baptism in the Holy Spirit is a separate, distinct, and usually subsequent experience that follows the experience of regeneration at conversion. Further, this position teaches that the initial evidence of receiving the baptism in the Spirit is speaking in tongues, as described in Acts 2 and Acts 10 and implied elsewhere. The gift of tongues as the initial evidence of receiving "the baptism" is viewed as necessary and important for the Spirit-filled Christian life. Following are quotes from the *Full Life Study Bible: An Interdenominational Study Bible for Pentecostal and Charismatic Christians*:

> The baptism in the Holy Spirit is an operation of the Spirit distinct and separate from his work of regeneration. . . One can be regenerated and indwelt by the Holy Spirit, but still not be baptized in the Holy Spirit. . . In the book of Acts, speaking in tongues as the Spirit gives utterance is the initial outward sign accompanying the baptism in the Holy Spirit. . . this should be the norm when receiving that baptism.[1]

---

[1] "Baptism in the Holy Spirit," *The Full Life Study Bible-NIV,* now re-titled *Life in the Spirit Bible-NIV* (Grand Rapids: Zondervan Publishing House, 1992, 2003), 1642.

On the other hand, the general position of the non-Pentecostal evangelical tradition is that the baptism in the Holy Spirit takes place at conversion and refers to the initial reception of the Holy Spirit when one is born again as implied in 1 Corinthians 12:13. John Stott well represents this point of view. In his widely regarded book, *Baptism and Fullness*, he contrasts the experience of the 120 in the upper room and the 3,000 who were converted on the Day of Pentecost:

> This distinction between the two companies, the 120 and the 3,000, is of great importance, because the *norm* for today must surely be the second group, the 3,000 . . . . The fact that the experience of the 120 was in two distinct stages was due simply to historical circumstances. They could not have received the Pentecostal gift before Pentecost. But those historical circumstances have long since ceased to exist. We live after the event of Pentecost, like the 3,000. With us, therefore, as with them, the forgiveness of sins and the "gift" or "baptism" of the Spirit are received together.[2]

Billy Graham concurs with this position. In his book, *The Holy Spirit*, he quotes W. Graham Scroggie to summarize his position and the position of most non-Pentecostal evangelicals:

> On the day of Pentecost all believers were, by the baptism of the Spirit, constituted the body of Christ, and since then every separate believer, every soul accepting Christ in simple faith, has in that moment and by that act been made partaker of the blessing of the baptism. It is not therefore a blessing which the believer is to seek and receive subsequent to the hour of his conversion.[3]

---

[2] John Stott, *Baptism and Fullness* (Downers Grove,IL: InterVarsity Press, 1975), 28.
[3] Billy Graham, *The Holy Spirit: Activating God's Power in Your Life*, Reissue edition (Nashville, TN: Thomas Nelson Publisher, 2000), 67.

Generally speaking, those who hold this view do not believe that tongues is a necessary or important gift of the Spirit, and some do not believe this gift is available at all today (see Chapter 6).

To the casual outside observer, these differences may not seem very important. However, to those individuals and churches that are at loggerheads with one another, feelings can run deep and can erupt into angry accusations and nasty church splits. Even where you find cordiality and cooperation between charismatic and non-charismatic leaders at meetings such as prayer breakfasts and evangelistic crusades, often the depth of partnership in Christ is minimal, and suspicions linger under the surface.

Very importantly, our theological differences *do* express themselves in practice — in what we preach; what we teach our people to expect; how we pray for our people; how we define and practice the "Spirit-filled" life. Unless, and until, we can agree on a theology of the Holy Spirit, leaders aren't going to feel comfortable exposing their people to the beliefs and practices of those who differ on these issues.

So who is right? Either or neither? Is there a solution to this theological impasse within Christ's body? To answer these questions, we must pray for the Spirit's guidance as we look to the Scriptures.

In the next few chapters I want to do several things: First, I want to prove by the Scriptures that there are *three phrases* used interchangeably in the New Testament to describe the same experience of the Spirit. They are: the promise of the Father, the gift of the Holy Spirit, and the baptism in the Holy Spirit. Second, I will try to define by the Scriptures what that experience is. And third, I will present a new paradigm or approach to understanding the baptism in the Holy Spirit, based on what we see in the Scriptures.

PF = GHS = BHS: One and the Same Experience

The New Testament equates three phrases and uses them interchangeably. They are "the promise of the Father," "the gift of the

Holy Spirit," and "the baptism in the Holy Spirit." This is substantiated by the following passages:

Matthew 3:11, Luke 24:49 and Acts 1:4–5. John the Baptist consistently pointed to One who would come and baptize believers in the Holy Spirit (Matthew 3:11, Mark 1:8, Luke 3:16). In John 1:33, he makes it clear who this One is — Jesus. Jesus said in Luke 24:49, "I am gong to send you what my Father has promised; but stay in the city until you have been clothed with power from on high." The *promise of the Father* is equated with being *baptized in the Holy Spirit* in Acts 1:4-5: "While staying with them, He ordered them not to leave Jerusalem, but to wait there for *the promise of the Father*. "This," He said, "is what you have heard from Me, for John baptized with water, but *you will be baptized with the Holy Spirit* not many days from now" (NRSV).

Acts 2:1-4, 2:16-17, 2:32-33. Peter explains that the outpouring of the Holy Spirit is the fulfillment of Joel 2:28–32: "In the last days, God says, I will pour out My Spirit on all people" (Acts 2:17). In Acts 2:33, Peter says of the Risen Christ that, "being therefore exalted at the right hand of God, and *having received from the Father the promise of the Holy Spirit, He has poured out this that you both see and hear*"(NRSV). Peter equates the outpouring of the Spirit at Pentecost with the promise of the Father to give the Holy Spirit as prophesied in Joel 2:28.

Acts 2:38-39. Peter equates the *promise of the Father* with the gift of the *Holy Spirit.* When asked by the hearers of his sermon what they should do, Peter answers: "Repent and be baptized, every one of you, in the name of Jesus Christ for the forgiveness of your sins. And you will *receive the gift of the Holy Spirit. The promise* is for you and your children and for all who are far off — for all whom the Lord our God will call." Then he opened their minds so they could understand the Scriptures.

Acts 10:44-47 and Acts 11:15-17. In these passages, the *gift of the Holy Spirit* and *the baptism in the Spirit* are equated. While Peter was preaching the first gospel message to Gentiles in the home of Cornelius, "the Holy Spirit fell upon all who had heard the message" (10:44). The Jewish Christians who had come with Peter "were astonished that *the gift of the Holy Spirit* had been poured out even on the Gentiles. For they heard them speaking in tongues and praising God" (10:45-46). Peter, in trying to explain the details of this event to the church in Jerusalem, said, "As I began to speak, the Holy Spirit came on them as he had come on us at the beginning. Then I remembered what the Lord had said: 'John baptized with water, but you will be *baptized with the Holy Spirit'*" (11:15-16). He continues, "So if God gave them *the same gift* as He gave us, who believed in the Lord Jesus Christ, who was I to think that I could oppose God?" (11:17).

It should be clear that the outpouring of the Holy Spirit that God promised in the Old Testament, and specifically through the prophet Joel in Joel 2:28-32, was fulfilled, beginning in Acts 2, when the Holy Spirit was poured out upon all who believed. As the Father promised, He gave the Holy Spirit to the church on the day of Pentecost. This gift of the Spirit, promised to all who believe, is also referred to as being baptized in the Holy Spirit.

So we ask again — *What is* the baptism in the Holy Spirit? What is the gift of the Spirit? Exactly what did the Father promise? Is this experience the *initial* gift of the Spirit, received by regeneration at conversion? Or, is it a *second* experience following regeneration and evidenced by speaking in tongues? Are these the only viable alternatives? Or is there another possibility, one that is broader, more general, and more inclusive of all the Holy Spirit's workings in the lives of individual believers and in churches?

Before we answer these questions, let's back up and see what expectations the disciples had concerning the coming of the Holy Spirit. First, let's look at the Old Testament to see what promises the Father made concerning the Holy Spirit. Then, we will take a look the teachings of Jesus to His followers to see what they would be expecting concerning the coming of the Spirit and His working in and among them.

Old Testament References Concerning the Coming of the Holy Spirit

In the Old Testament, the Holy Spirit anointed God's chosen leaders to serve in power. God's Spirit came upon prophets, judges, and kings to proclaim the Word of the Lord and to lead God's people. But the indwelling and empowering gift of the Spirit for *all* of God's people had to wait until the Day of Pentecost in the New Testament era. In **Numbers 11:28–29**, Joshua approached Moses with concern that seventy elders of Israel were prophesying by the power of the Holy Spirit. Moses said to Joshua, "Are you jealous for my sake? I wish that all the Lord's people were prophets and that the Lord would put His Spirit on them!"

In **Joel 2:28–32**, God proclaims through Joel that a time will come when the work of God's Spirit will be available to all people, old and young, women and men, free and slaves. The outpouring of the Spirit would result in visions, dreams, prophecies, and deliverance for all who call on the name of the Lord.

In **Jeremiah 31:31–34**, God promises that He will make a new covenant with His people in the future: "This is the covenant I will make with the house of Israel, . . . I will put my law in their minds and write it on their hearts. I will be their God and they will be my people." Although the Holy Spirit is not mentioned specifically in this passage, the characteristics of the new covenant God will make with His people in the future clearly correspond to the work of the Spirit in regeneration and indwelling, including the impartation of the new nature in Christ (See John 3:1–5 and 4:21–24; Galatians 5:15–22; and Ephesians 4:22–24).

In **Ezekiel 36:24-29**, God promises to restore His people. He will bring them back into the Promised Land after the exile period, and He will also give them new hearts and spirits: "I will give you a new heart and put a new spirit in you. I will remove from you your heart of stone and give you a heart of flesh. And I will put my Spirit in you and move you to follow my decrees . . . I will be your God." Here again God promises changes that correspond to the work of the Holy Spirit as described in the New Testament. God's people will be regenerated and indwelt by His Spirit; they will be given new hearts, a new nature that moves them to obey Him; they will also be cleansed from their sins.

These Old Testament passages point to a future coming of the Spirit upon God's people that would result in the impartation of a new nature, a new heart, a new spirit. The Spirit would indwell *all* of God's people, bringing them into a personal and fulfilling relationship with God. He would also motivate and empower them to obey and serve Him, and would give them supernatural revelations and gifts such as prophecies, dreams, and visions. These promises clearly point to New Testament works of the Spirit: regeneration, indwelling, empowerment, and spiritual gifts.

The Gospel of Luke and the Book of Acts

By way of review, we can look again at what Jesus had to say in the books of Luke and Acts. In **Luke 24:45–49**, Jesus opened their minds to understand the Scriptures: "This is what is written: The Christ will suffer and rise from the dead on the third day, and repentance and forgiveness of sins will be preached in his name to all nations, beginning at Jerusalem . . . I am going to send you *what my*

Father has promised; but stay in the city until you have been clothed with power from on high." In **Acts 1:4–5**, Jesus again tells His followers "to wait there for *the promise of the Father*. This . . . is what you have heard from me; for John baptized with water, but you will be *baptized with the Holy Spirit* not many days from now" (NRSV). And in **Acts 1:7–8**, Jesus informed them: "It is not for you to know the times or dates the Father has set by his own authority. But you will receive power when the Holy Spirit comes on you; and you will be my witnesses in Jerusalem, and in all Judea and Samaria, and to the ends of the earth."

Jesus commissioned His disciples, commanding them to preach the gospel to all nations. But prior to their going out, they must receive the Holy Spirit promised by God and given through Jesus. The Holy Spirit would come upon them in power and enable them to be witnesses for Christ starting in Jerusalem and going from there to the whole world. Here, the clear expectation is *empowerment for mission*.

The Gospel of John

Jesus made more references to the Spirit's coming in John's gospel than in any other. In **John 3:5–8**, Jesus answered, "I tell you the truth, no one can enter the kingdom of God unless he is born of water and the Spirit. Flesh gives birth to flesh, but the Spirit gives birth to spirit. You should not be surprised at my saying, 'You must be born again.' The wind blows wherever it pleases. You hear its sound, but you cannot tell where it comes from or where it is going. So it is with everyone born of the Spirit."

In this encounter with Nicodemus, Jesus makes it clear that unless one is born again (spiritually born, Spirit giving birth to spirit), one cannot enter the Kingdom of heaven. Being religious will not get us to heaven; one must be *spiritually* born.

John 4:7–14, 23–24 tells of Jesus' encounter with a Samaritan woman from whom he asked for a drink of water. The Samaritan woman asked, "How can you ask me for a drink?" Jesus answered her, "If you knew the gift of God and who it is that asks you for a drink, you would have asked him and he would have given you living water . . . Everyone who drinks this water will be thirsty again, but whoever drinks the water I give him will never thirst. Indeed, the water I give him will become in him a spring of water welling up to eternal life." He goes on to tell her that "a time is coming and has now come when the true worshipers will worship the Father in spirit and truth, for they are the kind of worshipers the Father seeks. God is spirit, and his worshipers must worship in spirit and in truth."

In this wonderful story, Jesus speaks of "living water" which we see in John 7:37–39 (see below) refers specifically to the Holy Spirit. He also speaks of true worship as that which is spiritual, i.e., in spirit and in truth. Because God is Spirit, if we wish to worship Him properly, we must worship Him spiritually. In the context of the entire Gospel of John, Jesus teaches that this spiritual worship of the Father is made possible by the regenerating work of the Spirit granted to those who profess faith in Christ.

In **John 7:37–39**, Jesus proclaims, "If anyone is thirsty, let him come to me and drink. Whoever believes in me, as the Scripture has said, streams of living water will flow from within him." By this he meant the Spirit, whom those who believed in him were later to receive. Up to that time the Spirit had not been given, since Jesus had not yet been glorified." Here, Jesus points to the Spirit who would indwell those who believe in Him. The Spirit would flow as rivers of living water from their hearts or innermost being. This would not take place until after Christ was glorified (e.g., until He had been crucified, risen, and ascended into heaven to take His place at God's right hand).

Jesus said in **John 14:12–13**: "I tell you the truth, anyone who has faith in me will do what I have been doing. He will do even greater things than these, because I am going to the Father. And I will do whatever you ask in my name, so that the Son may bring glory to the Father." Even though this passage does not explicitly speak of the Holy Spirit, it is not unreasonable to come to the view, especially in light of such passages as John 16:7 (listed below), that Jesus refers to the Holy Spirit as the source of power who will enable His followers to do the works that He does and to do even "greater works than these." It is advantageous for them that He go to the Father precisely because His going to the Father must precede the Holy Spirit's coming upon them.

In **John 14:15–17** Jesus taught, "If you love me, you will obey what I command. And I will ask the Father, and he will give you another Counselor to be with you for ever — the Spirit of truth. The world cannot accept him, because it neither sees him nor knows him. But you know him, for he lives with you and will be in you." The Holy Spirit will be with Christ's followers always. He will not only abide with us, but He will live in and among us, helping us and guiding us to truth. The person of the Holy Spirit makes Christ's presence real to us; thus Christ's words, "I am with you always" (Matthew 28:20).

Jesus taught in **John 14:25-26**: "All this I have spoken while still with you. But the Counselor, the Holy Spirit, whom the Father will send in my name, will teach you all things and will remind you of everything I have said to you." The Holy Spirit will teach us all things necessary in our Christian life and service and remind us of what Christ told us.

In **John 15:26** Jesus said, "When the Counselor comes, whom I will send to you from the Father, the Spirit of truth who goes out from the Father, he will testify about me." The Holy Spirit will testify on Christ's behalf. He will speak of Christ, and He will speak for Christ. And in **John 16:7–11** He said, "I tell you the truth: It is for your good that I am going away. Unless I go away, the Counselor will not come to you; but if I go, I will send him to you. When he comes, he will convict the world of guilt in regard to sin and righteousness and judgment: in regard to sin, because men do not believe in me; in regard to righteousness, because I am going to the Father, where you can see me no longer; and in regard to judgment, because the prince of this world now stands condemned." The Holy Spirit will be available to all believers simultaneously, whereas Christ, while on the earth was limited to one place. The Holy Spirit will vindicate God's truths concerning sin and righteousness and judgment. He will be the "Authenticator," authenticating the good news of the Gospel, the need for repentance, and escape from judgment.

In **John 16:12–15**, Jesus told His disciples that when "the Spirit of truth comes, he will guide you into all truth. He will not speak on his own; he will speak only what he hears, and he will tell you what is yet to come. He will bring glory to me by taking from what is mine and making it known to you." The Holy Spirit, the Spirit of truth, will guide Christ's followers into all truth and will reveal the mysteries and truths of God. No doubt this refers in large measure to the Spirit's work in inspiring the New Testament Scriptures as well as His ongoing guidance and inspiration for His people. He will glorify Jesus and reveal His truth and His will.

In **John 20:19–22**, Jesus said, "Peace be with you! As the Father has sent me, I am sending you." And with that he breathed on them and said, "Receive the Holy Spirit." In this passage, Jesus commissions His disciples to carry on His ministry and then empowers them to do so. Some believe that John is alluding to the coming of the Spirit at Pentecost, perhaps a prophetic and symbolic gesture to prepare them for the coming gift of the Spirit who would empower them to fulfill their mission. Others believe that Jesus really imparted the Spirit to these disciples (presumably ten of them, with the loss of Judas and the temporary absence of Thomas). In this case it is difficult to understand the relationship between what happened to these ten here and what happened to them when the Holy Spirit came at Pentecost. Many Pentecostals and charismatics assert that the disciples were *regenerated* in John 20 and then empowered and gifted with tongues and other gifts at Pentecost. However, the context of John 20:21–22 makes it clear that Jesus gave them the Spirit to *empower* them to fulfill their mission, not simply for regeneration.

Even if this passage does represent the first stage of a two-stage experience for them, it was an experience unique to them. If theirs was a two-stage experience of the Spirit — regeneration in John 20, followed by empowerment and gifts in Acts 2 — their experience was not duplicated by the 110 others in the upper room on the day of Pentecost, nor was it the experience of the next 3,000 who were converted and filled with the Spirit later that day. It is apparent that for these, the gifts, fruit, power, and many other evidences of the Spirit's operation were in evidence from their first experience of the Spirit.

The Gospel of Mark

Jesus said in Mark 16:17-18, "And these signs will accompany those who believe: In my name they will drive out demons; they will speak in new tongues; they will pick up snakes with their hands; and when they drink deadly poison, it will not hurt them at all; they will place their hands on sick people, and they will get well."

Although this passage is not found in the oldest and most reliable New Testament manuscripts, it is at least descriptive of the manifestations expected by the early Christians: speaking in tongues, healing, casting out demons, and miracles of protection from death by snakebite and poison.

Summary of Scriptures Pointing to the Holy Spirit's Coming

From these passages of Scripture we can summarize what the Holy Spirit's coming would mean for God's people, and what they might have been expecting. First, it meant **regeneration**, which includes spiritual birth, spiritual worship, the indwelling of the Holy Spirit. Second, there was the expectation for **empowering --** the work of the Holy Spirit that gives boldness and power, and that enables believers to witness and preach effectively. Third, they were anticipating **supernatural gifts**, including miraculous signs, healing, "greater works," prophecies, visions, and dreams. Then, **teaching and guidance** by the Spirit, reminding them of Christ's words, and guiding them into truth. And finally, **glorifying God**.

Returning Now to Our Original Question: "What is the Baptism in the Holy Spirit?"

Scripture uses the terms the baptism in the Holy Spirit, the gift of the Holy Spirit, and the promise of the Father interchangeably. Indeed, they are synonymous. Now what do they refer to? These terms are all-encompassing: they include all the Holy Spirit's workings described by the Old Testament prophecies, by John the Baptist, and by Jesus Christ. *The baptism or gift of the Holy Spirit then encompasses regeneration and indwelling of the Spirit, empowerment for witness, guidance into truth, spiritual gifts, worship (glorifying God), and all the other things the Holy Spirit does in the lives of believers and in the churches from the Day of Pentecost forward.*

It seems inconceivable to me that these terms could refer only to regeneration on the one hand, or only to a second experience of empowerment and gifting on the other. The promise of the Father (Old Testament prophecies) projected *both* the indwelling of the Spirit (Ezekiel 36:27; 37:14) *and* supernatural empowerment and gifts (Joel 2:23–29) for God's people. Jesus described regeneration, the indwelling of the Spirit, and Spirit-empowerment for ministry *all* as facets of the coming gift of the Spirit (John 7:37–39, Acts 1:8).

Certainly, the various workings of the Spirit are distinguishably different. The experience of being born again is different than being filled with the Spirit (see Chapter 5). The fruit of the Spirit (character traits in Galatians 5:22-23) differs from the gifts of the Spirit (Spirit-given abilities for service in 1 Corinthians 12:4–11 and Romans 12:6–8). Other very important but different workings of the Spirit include fellowship (Acts 2:41–44) and worship (Ephesians 5:18–20).

The question before us is this: Does the gift of the Holy Spirit or baptism in the Holy Spirit refer to only a "sliver" of the overall working of the Holy Spirit—whether the initial born-again experience or a subsequent filling and empowerment? Or, does this experience encompass the entire range of how the Holy Spirit works in the lives of individuals and churches from Pentecost forward? The Scriptural evidence makes it clear that the latter is true.

Chapter 2

When Are We Baptized with the Holy Spirit?—A Helpful Model

The general non-charismatic evangelical position is that the Holy Spirit baptizes us at conversion. It is an *initial* experience of the Holy Spirit, something equivalent to regeneration. The general Pentecostal/charismatic evangelical position says the Holy Spirit usually baptizes us sometime subsequent to conversion, and that this Spirit baptism experience is clearly distinct from being born again. As you can probably deduce from the preceding pages, I see inherent problems in both positions.

The Non-Charismatic Evangelical Position

First, let's look at the general non-charismatic evangelical position: the Holy Spirit baptism takes place at the time of conversion. This position has significant biblical support. Paul writes that "we were all baptized by one Spirit into one body . . . and we were all given the one Spirit to drink" (1 Corinthians 12:13). This certainly sounds like an experience at the beginning of the Christian life.

Some argue, however, that this baptism differs from the one that John the Baptist spoke of in Luke 3:16 (*He will baptize you with the Holy Spirit and with fire*) and Jesus spoke of in Acts 1:5 (*In a few days you will be baptized with the Holy Spirit).* They contend that 1 Corinthians 12:13 actually refers to the *Spirit* baptizing us into Christ's body, something quite distinct from the other scriptures that refer to *Jesus* baptizing us in the Holy Spirit. But this argument isn't very convincing. Just look at spiritual gifts: They are from *the Holy Spirit* in 1 Corinthians 12:7–11, but from *Christ* in Ephesians 4:11, and by inference from *God the Father* in 1 Corinthians 12:28.

Paul writes in 1 Corinthians 12:6 that "there are different kinds of working, but the *same God* works all of them in all men." We conclude from this that we run into trouble when we try to separate the operations of the three Persons of the Godhead as they relate to our spiritual experiences. It seems best, therefore, to conclude that the baptism *in* the Spirit by Jesus is synonymous with being baptized *by* the Holy Spirit—*God* at work in us.

Still, when we try to make the baptism in the Holy Spirit synonymous with the initial experience of regeneration at conversion, we miss something. What about the clear Scriptural evidences of receiving the Spirit that go *beyond* regeneration; namely, power and boldness to witness; and spiritual gifts, including miraculous ones such as healing, prophecy, and speaking in tongues? The problem with equating the baptism in the Spirit with regeneration is that we can wind up with a pretty anemic life in the Spirit.

We find this especially true when we contrast our experience with what we see in the Book of Acts after the Spirit came. By accepting this limited definition of the baptism in the Spirit, far too many of us Christians have settled for so much less than the Scriptures promise us. We thus diminish our expectancy of the Spirit's power and other supernatural manifestations of His presence. This becomes serious when we realize that our level of expectancy has a lot to do with what we actually experience. Jesus said, "According to your faith will it be done to you" (Matthew 9:29). The appeal that regeneration/salvation is the greatest miracle of all (which, of course, is true), should not in any way lessen our desire to see further workings of the Spirit to build Christ's body or to evangelize the lost. Jesus longs to hear passionate heart cries for His kingdom to come and His will to be done on earth as in heaven. If this is truly our heart, we soon realize then that we need more of His Spirit, not less.

In short, we find the option that the baptism in the Spirit refers only to an initial experience in the Spirit inadequate. It encompasses some, but certainly not all, that the prophets, John the Baptist, and Jesus told us to expect when the Spirit comes.

The Pentecostal/Charismatic Evangelical Position

Most Pentecostals and charismatics believe that the baptism in the Holy Spirit is a *second experience* generally evidenced by the manifestation of speaking in tongues. This position has one strong point in its favor: It *does* embrace the workings of the Holy Spirit beyond regeneration, which the first position diminishes and sometimes even ignores. Not only does the second position emphasize these further workings of the Holy Spirit; it also encourages born-again believers to desire and seek them earnestly, which often results in Christian life and experiences that more closely resemble those we read about in the book of Acts.

There are problems, however, with this view as well. There is insufficient biblical evidence to warrant the belief that the baptism in the Holy Spirit is a *second* experience. It seems that every attempt to make a case for it has a flaw. For example, if John the Baptist and Jesus referred to a *second* experience, how did they refer to the *first* one in contrast to it? Why did they never say, "Before you can be baptized with the Holy Spirit, you must *first* be born again"? Why would they point people to a *second* experience before they had received the *first* one?

The Scriptures do not teach, *as a normative pattern*, the baptism in the Spirit as a second experience that follows conversion. To be sure, in the book of Acts, we see times when believers experienced the Holy Spirit's fullness in stages. We see one example in Acts 8:12–17, where many Samaritans turned to Christ and got baptized in response to Philip's preaching of the gospel. When the apostles in Jerusalem got wind of this, they sent Peter and John, who "prayed for them that they might receive the Holy Spirit, because the Holy Spirit had not yet come upon any of them"(Acts 8:15–16). When Peter and John laid their hands on them, the Samaritans received the Spirit.

Another example is seen in Acts 19:1–7, where Paul came upon some *disciples*. When he asked them whether they had received the Holy Spirit, they replied, "No, we have not even heard that there is a Holy Spirit." Paul had to instruct them about Christian baptism because at that point they had only received John's baptism for repentance. He explained to them that "John's baptism was a baptism of repentance," and that John had told the people to believe in Jesus. So after baptizing them, Paul laid hands on them, and "the Holy Spirit came on them, and they spoke in tongues and prophesied."

There's just no denying it—these are clear examples of a two-stage experience in the Holy Spirit. Yet, we do find equally clear passages that describe believers receiving the Spirit's fullness—including regeneration, tongues, empowerment, etc.—as an *initial* experience. We find the first of these in Acts 2 on the Day of Pentecost. One hundred twenty followers of Jesus had been instructed to wait for the promise of the Father, for their empowerment from on high (Luke 24:49); they would be baptized with the Holy Spirit (Acts 1:5) and receive power to be His witnesses (Acts 1:8). Suddenly, "All of them were filled with the Holy Spirit, and began to speak in other tongues as the Spirit enabled them" (Acts 2:4).

Some have argued that what these believers actually experienced on Pentecost was a *second* experience after they initially received the Spirit in John 20:21–22 when Jesus commissioned His disciples and breathed on them saying, "Receive the Holy Spirit." If this were true of the disciples who were with Jesus in John 20:21–22, it was *not* true for the rest of the one hundred twenty who were *not* there at that time. For the rest of them, their first experience in personally receiving the gift of the Spirit took place on the Day of Pentecost.

The *second*, even more conclusive example of the baptism in the Spirit referring to an initial experience also took place on the day of Pentecost. Peter, now Spirit-empowered, preaches a sermon accompanied with signs and wonders. This results in the conversion of *3,000* people who no doubt entered the Spirit-filled life right then.

We find a *third* clear example in Acts 10 in the home of Cornelius, a God-fearing Gentile (this was the first time the gospel was preached to the Gentiles). Acts 10:44 tells us, "While Peter was still speaking these words, the Holy Spirit came on all who heard the message." The Jewish believers were amazed "that the *gift of the Holy Spirit* had been poured out even on the Gentiles. For they heard them speaking in tongues and praising God" (Acts 10:45-46).

So let's summarize: On the one hand, we see biblical examples where the baptism in /gift of the Holy Spirit happened in two stages; on the other hand, we see biblical examples where the baptism in/gift of the Spirit seemed to happen all at once. Since we find clear examples of the Holy Spirit working in varying ways, we must conclude that no basis exists for claiming that either one of these positions is *normative* for all believers.

We can say that both a one-stage reception of the Spirit (as at Pentecost and in Acts 10) is *normal, and* a two-stage reception of the Spirit (as in Acts 8 and Acts 19) is *normal.* The reception of the Spirit happened both ways in Scripture. And, because it happened both ways in Scripture, and because Scripture teaches no specific pattern elsewhere with regard to being baptized in the Holy Spirit, *we must conclude that neither one-stage nor two-stage receptions of the Spirit are the normative way.* To clarify, it is biblically inaccurate to teach that the baptism in or gift of the Holy Spirit is *necessarily* synonymous with an initial experience; sometimes the fullness of that experience happened in stages. It is equally inaccurate to teach that it is *necessarily* a subsequent or additional experience to conversion; sometimes the full dimensions of that experience were evident from the outset.

A Helpful Model: "Unwrapping" the Gift of the Spirit

In teaching, I use an illustration that many have found helpful in providing them a better understanding of what the gift of the Spirit is and when we receive it. I have seen God use this model to "turn the light on" in many minds regarding this subject. He has used it to tear down walls between many so-called "haves" and "have-nots," building bridges of fellowship and understanding to replace barricades of tension, mistrust, and division. Many people, after hearing this teaching on the baptism with the Spirit, have sighed with relief, and some have even wept as they release pent-up feelings of confusion, doubt, spiritual inferiority, and self-condemnation. Persons with spiritual roots in both charismatic and non-charismatic evangelical churches have found benefit and encouragement. This model provides a theological umbrella under which we can come together in genuine unity and partnership.

This approach has not only been effective in the churches that I have pastored but also in other churches that have used it. One example, from Rev. Keith Cerk, Pastor at First Baptist Church of Waukegan, Illinois: "Your presentation of the ministry of the Holy Spirit has helped me and the people of our church a great deal. We have people come to our church from a very wide range of theological backgrounds, from Southern Baptist to Pentecostal, as well as the unchurched – and your approach makes sense to them all. Without going to divisive doctrinal extremes, it allows us to open up to more vibrant life and new ministries in the Holy Spirit without making us feel weird or goofy." Keith's church has been experiencing significant renewal in a tough-to-reach inner-city type area near Chicago.

The particular model I use derives from Acts 2:38, where Peter concludes a powerful evangelistic message on the Day of Pentecost. The Spirit convicts the people of their sins, and they become desperate to know what to do next. Peter responds, "Repent and be baptized, every one of you in the name of Jesus Christ for the forgiveness of your sins. And *you will receive the gift of the Holy Spirit.*"

Imagine you have just heard the gospel, responded to it, and received Jesus Christ as your Savior and Lord. Now picture God handing you a big gift-wrapped box called ***"THE HOLY SPIRIT."*** The Holy Spirit has come to you as a gift because of your faith in Christ. You go ahead and unwrap it and peer inside. Right on top, the first thing you see is a package labeled *Born Again.* It is the gift of regeneration. Your faith opens this miraculous gift — the veil is lifted and the Spirit comes into your life. God's Spirit bears witness to your spirit that you have become a child of God (see Romans 8:15–16).

But you don't stop there because you see that within the large box, which is already your gift, there are *more gift-wrapped packages*. You look down deeper and pull one out labeled ***"Character of Christ."*** Unwrapping this package, you encounter the fruit of the Spirit: "Love, joy, peace, patience, kindness, goodness, faithfulness, gentleness, and self-control" (Galatians 5:22). The Holy Spirit begins the lifelong process of making you like Jesus. Your prayer becomes, "Lord, I want to become more like You. Fill me with your Holy Spirit, so that I can show people what You're really like and so I can live the way you want me to live."

Looking inside the Holy Spirit box again, you come across another package called ***Spiritual Gifts***. Well, this one looks interesting. There's a note right on it that says *Customized just for you.* Wow, this one is tailor-made for you personally because the Holy Spirit has an assortment of gifts and distributes them as He wills to each child of God. As you unwrap it, you begin to understand and experience gifts of the Holy Spirit that enable you, as an individual, to serve Christ with power and effectiveness.

This "Spiritual Gifts" package may include one or more of the supernatural gifts, such as prophecy, healing, words of wisdom and knowledge, and speaking in tongues (1 Corinthians 12:8–11).[4] It may also include more natural abilities you already possess but that are

---

[4] See Chapter 6 for a lengthy discussion on the gift of speaking in tongues.

now endued with the Holy Spirit's power, things like service, giving, administration, leadership, and teaching (see Romans 12:6–8). As we yield ourselves to the Spirit's leading, we can become powerful instruments through whom He ministers to others.

What happens if you fail to "unwrap" this "Spiritual Gifts" package?

If you are part of a church or tradition that doesn't teach much about spiritual gifts, you might just choose to ignore it. If you don't expect the supernatural spiritual gifts, have never experienced them yourself, do not know anyone who has, and are told by your church that these are not available today, would you be likely to want to explore this package? Would you be hungry for spiritual gifts? Probably not. Sadly, many Christians deprive themselves from being more powerfully used by God simply because they disregard their spiritual gifts and refuse to seek after new ones. Jesus said, "According to your faith will it be done to you" (Matthew 9:29).

Nevertheless, here is this package and a lot more besides — all waiting in this large gift box called the Holy Spirit. God watches, waits, longs for us to "unwrap" *all* the packages He's given us in this wonderful box. As Paul the apostle wrote, "Praise be to the *God* and Father of our Lord Jesus Christ, who *has blessed us* in the heavenly realms *with every spiritual blessing in Christ"* (Ephesians 1:3). What does "every spiritual blessing" mean for us? It means *every* spiritual blessing in Christ is currently available. None is relegated to the pages of biblical history. God has blessed *us*, the church of the 21st century, with *every* spiritual blessing He *ever* gave His church, either in the early church or since then. These blessings—every one of them—are available for our use and activated for us by this glorious gift of the Holy Spirit. Nothing is automatic, however. We must appreciate the excellence of these blessings and workings of the Holy Spirit and appropriate them *by faith*. We must dig into the box, take out all the packages, and "unwrap" them.

What else can we find in this amazing box? More wonderful things! We can find a package labeled "***Koinonia,***" the Greek word used in the New Testament for fellowship, sharing, and participation. The fellowship of the Holy Spirit (see Acts 2:41, 4:32) is a splendid gift that joins our hearts in loving communion with God and with our brothers and sisters in Christ. This gift makes us aware of our full acceptance as members of God's family. Its depth motivates us to share the deepest parts of our being with one another and to carry one another's heaviest burdens. And its breadth, encompassing the entire planet, enables us to find instant "family" in the Holy Spirit with Christian people wherever we go. With this gift unwrapped, we cannot be *lone ranger* Christians. We are Christ's body—together, toughing it out in this world; together advancing His kingdom on earth; and together waiting eagerly for His coming and doing what we can to hasten it.

Let's unwrap another one! There's one called "***Power to Witness***." Opening this one, we experience an empowering of the Holy Spirit to be witnesses for Christ and proclaimers of His gospel (see Acts 1:8, 4:31).

And here's another one labeled "***Praise and Thanksgiving.***" One result of being filled with the Holy Spirit is that we become grateful—even enthusiastic—worshipers. Like David in the Psalms and like Paul and Barnabas as they sang songs of praise in prison, we love praising Him. Paul the apostle says, ". . . *be filled with the Spirit.* Speak to one another with *psalms, hymns, and spiritual songs. Sing and make music in your heart to the Lord, always giving thanks to God* the Father for everything, in the name of our Lord Jesus Christ" (Ephesians 5:18–20).

We could keep on going: there's a package called "***Guidance,***" another one labeled "***Revelation***." God wants us to unwrap, appropriating by faith, *all* the "blessing" packages he has already given us in this box called ***THE HOLY SPIRIT***.

In the Old Testament, the Israelites ventured across the Jordan River and into the Promised Land. God had given them the land and it was now theirs—"*See, I have given you this land*" (Deuteronomy 1:8). But the Israelites were not to sit passively on the river bank after crossing over. They had to move into the land and take by faith what God had given them—"*Go in and take possession of the land*" (Deuteronomy *1:8)*.

And so it is with the Spirit-filled life. Our part is to receive the gift of the Holy Spirit and to open *every one of the packages* God has given us. In order to discover all He has made available to us in spiritual workings, manifestations, and gifts of the Holy Spirit, we've got to seek His face and study His Word. Our heart's attitude should always be, "God, I want everything you have for me. . . I want to make a difference in my world for you." If ever the full working of the Holy Spirit in and through Christians and churches was needed, it is today! It is inconceivable that God would want His people to be powerless in a world that is increasingly being challenged and assaulted by the powers of darkness.

People Differ In Their Experiences

This model of the "The Gift of the Holy Spirit" as a box filled with gift-wrapped packages helps us understand how our experiences in the Holy Spirit can be so varied. Some people appear to experience every working of the Spirit at once. They are born again and seem to be "zapped" by the Holy Spirit with gifts, fruit, power right at the outset of their Christian experience. On the other hand, others develop more gradually, seeming to experience the Spirit's work in stages. All believers receive *The Holy Spirit* at conversion, but we often seem to unwrap the packages inside at different times and in different sequences. The point is that God intends for each of us to open *all* the packages and appropriate them by faith, praying that we receive *the fullness* of His Gift of the Holy Spirit.

An Encouraging Approach

This approach to understanding the gift of the Holy Spirit, or the baptism in the Holy Spirit, has the power to encourage us all. First, it encourages us by the fact that *we Christians have all been given the gift of the Holy Spirit,* filled with at least some packages that are uniquely customized for us, to help us know God better, to grow in Him, and to serve Him more effectively. No "haves-versus-have-nots" exists; we all have "the Gift." Now we no longer find any basis for judging ourselves or others by a particular experience. *All* of the packages in the box represent normal, beneficial, desirable workings of the Holy Spirit. But, for a variety of reasons, we do not experience them uniformly. Rather, we experience them in differing ways, at differing times, and to differing degrees.

Second, this way of looking at these issues encourages us by freeing us from the pressure of feeling like our experience must conform to a set pattern or norm. God doesn't make us all the same. We are not identical clones but unique and beloved individuals. We are flat out wrong if we erect doctrinal or experiential hurdles and barriers that the Word of God does not erect. We are also wrong when we absolutize our own experiences—or lack thereof—and judge everyone else by them.

Our experiences in the Holy Spirit can be *normal*, but not necessarily *normative.* As wonderful as they might be to us, that doesn't give us license to establish them as a norm or pattern of experience that must be precisely repeated in the lives of every other Christian. Again, we should never try to interpret the Scriptures by our experiences; rather, we should interpret our experiences by the Scriptures.

Third, this model encourages us to appropriate by faith everything God has given us. We all need to continue appropriating the fullness of the Holy Spirit. Sometimes this is demonstrated in gradual and steady growth, and sometimes it is demonstrated in momentous breakthroughs. Whatever the case, not one of us can rightly say we have all of the Spirit's fullness. Who can honestly say, "I have everything the Holy Spirit has to offer. I am completely Spirit-filled at all times!"? Certainly not I! In truth, Jesus Christ is the only one who can legitimately make this claim.

We all need to grow: Some of us need to focus our growth toward love, joy, peace—the fruit of the Spirit. Others of us haven't "unwrapped" the spiritual gifts package; remember, Paul wrote in 1 Corinthians 14:1, "Make love your aim, *and earnestly desire the spiritual gifts"* (RSV). Many of us need to repent of our lone-ranger mentality and open the *Koinonia* (fellowship) package. Lots more of us need to open the *Praise and Thanksgiving* package. And who cannot use more of the *Power to Witness* package?

The point is that we all need to press in and press on, seeking God for more and more of Him and His Spirit. It is true that in Christ, we *have been* blessed in Him with every special blessing (Ephesians 1:3). But He wants us to take initiative—hungering, thirsting, reaching out for a more dynamic, energetic, expectant faith and for more fruitful lives. He wants our faith to move us ever further into the *promised land* of life in the Spirit, appropriating and acting on what He has already given us.

Some glorious day, we will meet Christ face to face, and His fullness will be realized in each one of us. Until that day, we must press on—there is always more!

Chapter 3

"There's More!"

Whether we consider ourselves charismatics, non-charismatics, or something in-between, I think if we are all honest, we will acknowledge that there is more available within the gift of the Holy Spirit than we have personally experienced. We may generally walk in the power and victory of the Holy Spirit, but none of us has arrived, and *we won't until* we reach our final destination and meet our Lord face to face.

In the last chapter, we saw a model that helps us understand what it means to receive the gift of the Holy Spirit. We learned that the Holy Spirit works in different ways in the lives of different people, that what is a *normal* experience (biblically supported), is not necessarily a *normative* experience (biblically commanded). We saw in the Book of Acts the gift or baptism in the Spirit sometimes was received in fullness from the outset and at other times in stages. As we honestly look around us today, we find that this is the case in our time, too. Some people seem to experience a release in the Spirit or filling with the Spirit in most every dimension of His working right from the outset of their Christian experience. Others seem to have stages of release or filling. These go along for a while, and then suddenly they have a spiritual breakthrough into an area of the Spirit's working that they hadn't previously experienced to such a degree.

Why the Stages?

As I look at my own spiritual pilgrimage, it is clear that my Holy Spirit discovery journey has been in stages. During my late junior and early senior years of college, I was on a holy quest to find the meaning and purpose of life. I took a course entitled "The Life and Ministry of Jesus" the first semester of my senior year. This led me to read the New Testament and books written by German theologians. As I read, I experienced a growing fascination related to Jesus Christ. He became my hero, in a sense, and I wanted to be like Him. I didn't realize at that time that the Bible's miracle accounts were true, and I didn't believe that Christ rose from the dead. Still, I searched. One day, much to my surprise, Jesus Christ stepped out of the pages of the New Testament right into my heart. I was gloriously and profoundly converted; I was dramatically born again by the Spirit of God. There was no question in my mind that I had received the Holy Spirit—God's love and presence were so strong in my life that I tingled all over and wept for joy.

About two years later I heard about speaking in tongues. Out of curiosity, I read a book about the subject. Consequently, in the privacy of my own seminary apartment, I asked for and received a prayer language. After this experience, I noticed an increased anointing when I preached and a greater delight than ever before in singing praises to God.[5]

A few years after that, I experienced on a deeper level the meaning of Christian fellowship. Until then, I had been a pretty independent Christian. But a real breakthrough of the Spirit in my life came when He truly knit me into a body of believers and taught me what Christian *family* is about.

In more recent years, I've seen breakthroughs in the area of Holy Spirit anointing for leadership, in the area of giving, and also in the area of ministering in the Holy Spirit's gifts (like prophecy, words of knowledge, discernment, and healing) as I pray for people. And all along I have continued to grow and mature in the *fruit* of the Spirit.

---

[5] See Chapter 7 for a more lengthy discussion of my personal experience with the gift of tongues.

Why have I developed in stages? I suppose all of us develop spiritually over time. We become more Christ-like (hopefully!), and our faith grows as we learn to trust God and obey Him through the years. But I am not talking here about growth areas where we all develop over time. Our focus here is the reasons why some of us develop in stages, showing steady growth in some areas, while in other areas we may need major or momentous breakthroughs.

Reason #1: Inadequate Instruction

In Acts 19, Paul asked the disciples he met outside Ephesus whether or not they had received the Holy Spirit when they first believed. Their answer: "No, we have not even heard that there is a Holy Spirit" (19:2). They had only received John's baptism of repentance and had not been baptized as Christians in the Name of Jesus. Possibly, these men weren't yet Christians at all, but they are described as "disciples." At any rate, they had not been adequately taught; they needed to know more about Christ, Christian baptism, and the Holy Spirit. Following more adequate instruction, they were baptized and ready to receive the gift of the Holy Spirit in fullness. As Paul placed his hands on them, "the Holy Spirit came upon them, and they spoke in tongues and prophesied" (19:6). The obvious problem these Ephesian disciples had is the same problem that many believers have today: Many of us have been *inadequately instructed!*

Inadequate instruction is one of the greatest reasons so many Christians do not experience more of the Spirit's fullness. We think we have all there is, or all we need. Paul wrote about this need for awakening to the *MORE* that is available to us as believers in Christ:

> I keep asking that the God of our Lord Jesus Christ, the glorious Father, may give you the Spirit of wisdom and revelation, so *that you may know Him better.* I pray also *that the eyes of your heart may be enlightened* in order *that you may know* the *hope* to which he has called you, the *riches of his glorious inheritance* in the saints, and *his incomparably*

> *great power for us who believe.* That power is like the working of His mighty strength, which he exerted in Christ when he raised Him from the dead and seated him at his right hand in the heavenly realms (Ephesians 1:17–20).

Just think about that passage. Paul prays that believers—yes, that includes us!—will have their spiritual perceptions awakened to know and experience God better, to understand and appropriate the blessings God has given us in Christ and in His gift of the Holy Spirit. Imagine if *all* of us Christians could perceive and receive His "incomparably great power" available to us. Watch out, world! Here comes the church! Wouldn't we turn this world upside down for Christ as the early Christians did? Just think: Resurrection power! Holy Spirit power! We need to know there's more, cry out for more, open our hearts and minds to more, and yield more of ourselves to Him—"More, Lord!" should be our cry.

I remember reading a story about Charles Spurgeon, the great preacher in England whose sermons once circled the globe. He was visiting the home of an apparently destitute elderly woman who was terribly sick. She didn't have the money for proper care and was lying on her bed when Spurgeon came to see her. After chatting a bit, he browsed around the small room, looking at her pictures and knickknacks. Suddenly, he stopped at a peculiar framed document on her wall. He asked, "What is this?" The frail little woman answered, "I took care of a wealthy woman in her later years, and she gave it to me as something to remember her by." After examining the document more closely, Spurgeon exclaimed, "Do you know what this document is? Why, this is the trust deed to her estate!"

Here the little lady had been living for years as a pauper—sick and without proper care, in a run-down little house—when all the while she was RICH! She could have had a beautiful home, the best medical attention, all she ever could have dreamed of. She was rich, true. But the only trouble was, she didn't realize it. She had not been instructed properly, and therefore she did not receive the benefit of what had been given her.

In my own experience, had someone properly instructed me when I was first converted, I feel certain I would have opened several more of those "wrapped packages" in the Holy Spirit Gift Box much sooner. I really knew nothing at all about spiritual gifts; nor had I experienced *koinonia* (fellowship in the Spirit) or Spirit-led praise and worship, to name a few. I'm sure this is true for many others, as well.

You may be in a church that doesn't teach about these things, and you haven't come across any book on the subject. Or, maybe you've been poisoned against or "spooked" by some of the more dramatic manifestations of the Holy Spirit. Your knowledge is incomplete or inaccurate, and consequently you haven't been ready to open those packages. Perhaps you've left the package entitled "*Spiritual Gifts*" still wrapped and forgotten in the bottom of the box, and now it's time to take it out and open it!

Reason #2: Lack of Desire

It is quite possible—and, looking at the state of the church in America, even prevalent—to be completely satisfied with the measure of Holy Spirit life and power we currently experience. Often we lack desire because we don't have a significant degree of spiritual purpose in our lives.

Once, a man decided to take a tour of an oil refinery. As the guide led him on the tour of the plant, he saw where the crude oil came in, where it was refined, and how they got rid of the impurities in the oil. The plant was spotlessly clean with state-of-the-art technology and equipment. And the office was a showcase of beautiful yet functional furnishings. The man was impressed, but as the tour ended, he had a question: "Hey, wait a minute! Did you forget to show me the place from which you *export* the oil?"

"Export!?" the tour guide replied quizzically. "Why, it takes all the oil we make just to run the plant!"

Perhaps you chuckle at this little story. Yet sadly, it underscores a condition of many Christians and churches that is anything but humorous. Far too many of us are content with just enough of the Holy Spirit to ensure our entrance into heaven, or just enough to enable us to cope with the problems in our personal lives. "Export!?" you may ask. "It takes all the Holy Spirit power I have to cope with the pressures in my own life. Or, in the case of the church, "It takes all the Holy Spirit our church has to keep the doors open." In fact, sometimes we are so accustomed to the way things are that we don't even recognize when we live in abysmal spiritual poverty. Like the oil refinery that had *the look* of success, we build awe-inspiring edifices and give our impressive tours to visitors. But where's the oil for exporting?

When we as Christians or churches get to that place, we need a "wake-up call." We need an *awakening to spiritual purpose*! Several years ago, I did a study of the Scriptures to see if I could find a corresponding relationship between having spiritual purpose and being filled with the Spirit. I must tell you that my findings *amazed* me. In virtually *every* instance I found that *the Holy Spirit came in power solely in conjunction with spiritual purpose.* Study the following passages, and see for yourself the relationship between the Spirit's power and spiritual purpose:

- Ephesians 5:15–18 "Be very careful, then, how you live — not as unwise but as wise, *making the most of every opportunity* because the days are evil. Therefore do not be foolish but understand what the Lord's will is. Do not get drunk on wine which leads to debauchery. Instead, *be filled with the Spirit.*"
- Acts 5:28–32 When religious leaders ordered Peter and the other apostles not to teach about Jesus Christ, Peter replied: "We must obey God rather than men . . . We are witnesses of these things, and so is *the Holy Spirit, whom God has given to those who obey Him.*"

- Acts 1:8 "But you will receive power when *the Holy Spirit* comes on you; and you will be *my witnesses . . . .*"
- Acts 4:31 "After they had prayed, the place where they were meeting was shaken. And *they were all filled with the Holy Spirit and spoke the Word of God boldly.*"
- John 20:21–22 "Again Jesus said, '. . . As the Father has sent me, *I am* sending *you.*' And with that He breathed on them and said, '*Receive the Holy Spirit'.*"
- Isaiah 61:1–3 *"The Spirit of the Sovereign Lord is on me, because* the Lord has anointed me to *preach* good news to the poor. He has sent me to *bind up* the brokenhearted, to *proclaim* freedom for the captives and release from darkness for the prisoners . . . to *comfort* all who mourn and *provide* for those who grieve in Zion . . ."

As you can see, the fullness of the Holy Spirit is always given in conjunction with spiritual purpose. Spiritual purpose for Christians is characterized by such things as having an earnest desire to please God; to live a life worthy of Him; to exalt Him and bring Him glory; to draw others to Him; to show forth His power and love to a desperately needy yet skeptical world.

One major problem in our society is our extreme narcissism. To a frightening degree, this malady has carried over into many churches. Large numbers have come to see the filling of the Holy Spirit as a means to spiritual thrills and experiences. "Touch me," "bless me," "fill me," "thrill me," "heal me" . . . me—Me—ME!!! Not that God is reluctant to touch us and bless us; He wants to. But He longs to see in us hearts that seek Him and His Kingdom first. So many of us are so preoccupied with ourselves, with our experiences and pleasures and comforts, that we scarcely if ever think or pray in terms of our making a difference in this world for Christ.

The Holy Spirit was *not* given to create "bless me clubs" for spiritual elites. He didn't come to entertain us with thrills, or to satisfy our appetites for more intense experiences, or to gratify our inclinations toward self-aggrandizement, or to flatter us with increased spiritual prowess, or to indulge our egos in any way.

He was *not* given for emotional ecstasy. He wants to produce DYNAMIC DISCIPLESHIP and EFFECTIVE ENABLEMENT! He wants to reproduce, in and through us, the life, character, and ministry of Jesus Christ.

We cannot expect a release into the Spirit's fullness unless we have enough spiritual purpose to want to serve Christ in the power of the Holy Spirit for the glory of God the Father. Our desires and motives are paramount to God.

Reason #3: God Works in Us Individually

You may be frustrated in your spiritual life, particularly with the measure of the Spirit's power and giftedness you have been experiencing. Perhaps the reason isn't that you need more instruction or that you lack desire. You may have read everything you can get your hands on and prayed earnestly for more of God's Spirit to be released in your life. You've waited and waited for a breakthrough, but it still hasn't come. You just don't seem to have the freedom to worship, or power to witness, or spiritual gifts to serve that you want so badly.

You shouldn't feel like there is something wrong with you or that you are a "second-class citizen" in God's kingdom. If your motives are right—to serve Christ and glorify God—then God is pleased with your heart. Thank Him for what you *do* have, and trust Him that you are where He wants you to be for now. That doesn't mean you should give up your desire for more; God blesses those who hunger and thirst for His kingdom and His righteousness. But trust Him, and don't let your holy discontentment turn into self-condemnation or cynicism about the Holy Spirit, or mistrust in your heavenly Father.

Remember, God says: "For my thoughts are not your thoughts, neither are your ways my ways . . . As the heavens are higher than the earth, so are my ways higher than your ways and my thoughts than your thoughts" (Isaiah 55:8–9). He is sovereign; He knows us as the unique individuals that we are. Because He has unique and specific plans for each of us, He works in our lives in different ways and at different times.

Like a loving parent with a child, our heavenly Father loves us and wants to meet our needs. We may rest assured that He wants to use us for His Kingdom's work more than we want to be used. Jesus promises, "If you then . . . know how to give good gifts to your children, *how much more will your Father in heaven give the Holy Spirit to those who ask Him*" (Luke 11:13). And Paul the apostle assures us, "*He who did not spare His own Son*, but gave Him up for us all—*how will He not also, along with Him, graciously give us all things*" (Romans 8:32).

God rarely chooses to explain why He does things the way He does. If He did, we wouldn't need to trust Him! Yet, sometimes He totally surprises us with unexpected Holy Spirit breakthroughs in our lives. At other times, however, it seems all He has to say is "Wait," or worse, He seems to say nothing at all! Remember, Jesus likened the Holy Spirit to the wind, signifying a certain "unpredictability" in the way He works. This is definitely true from our human vantage point.

We may wonder why "so-and-so" had some astounding spiritual encounter that blessed her socks off while we still just struggle along. I will never forget the time, before I married Cheri, when I heard a frantic pounding at my seminary apartment door. I got up quickly, opened the door, and there she was—a sobbing wreck. I hadn't known her long, but she had always seemed like a relatively normal person. So it distressed me to see her this way. I assumed someone had just died. "What's the matter? What happened?" I asked. "I didn't *fall down*! I didn't *fall down*!" she bawled. "Everyone around me fell down . . . but *I didn't*!"

As the story unfolded, I learned that she had gone to a revival meeting, and everyone the evangelist touched had "fallen under the power" of the Spirit. It relieved me greatly to learn that no one had died, but her behavior mystified me. "Why did you want to fall on the floor?" I asked. She didn't really know except that everyone else had fallen on the floor and she felt something must be wrong with her, that she was missing out on a major blessing from God because of it.

Cheri was still a young Christian with substantial rejection issues. It took quite some time to calm her down and convince her that she was okay, that God still loved her, and that this "inability" to experience a particular spiritual manifestation had no bearing on her status as a full-fledged citizen of God's kingdom.

As members of Christ's body, we need to be *very careful* to avoid attaching undue prominence to spiritual experiences or manifestations. This is *especially* true when we can find neither explicit nor even implicit substantiation for them in the Scriptures. "Falling under the power" of the Spirit[6] may be an experience that God uses to refresh or heal people (I was once "melted" to the floor in a Christian gathering and giggled for the next three days!). But we have no real basis in Scripture for viewing such experiences as normative or as a basis for comparison with other Christians. What is important and desirable here is the refreshing and fullness of God's Spirit. When we chase particular experiences, rather than seek the Holy Spirit Himself, we will run into trouble—nearly always.

Again, we don't always, or even often, know the "why" of God's dealings in our lives. Christian maturity allows for the element of mystery related to our awesome God whose wisdom and ways are

---

[6] Also variously called "overcome by the Spirit," "resting in the Spirit," being "slain in the Spirit," and "falling before the Lord," this is a spiritual experience where a person falls to the floor during a personal encounter with God's power. Described as a human response to the manifestation of God's Spirit, it is likened to incidents in the Bible where God's presence was accompanied by such phenomenon as trembling, physical weakness, falling, or even deep sleep. Involuntary falling resulting from God's overwhelming presence can be seen in such places as Daniel 8:17–18; 10:8-11, Ezekiel 1:28, Acts 9:3–4, Revelation 1:17. It generally occurs in Pentecostal or Charismatic meetings through the laying on of hands. It was also quite common in early American Methodism. The great evangelist, Charles Finney, said in his autobiography, "I observed a woman … supposing that she was in a fainting fit… After lying in a speechless state about sixteen hours, Miss G___'s mouth was opened, and a new song was given her. She was taken from the horrible pit of miry clay, and her feet were set on a rock; and it was true that many saw it and feared" (from *The Autobiography of Charles G. Finney*, New York: A.S. Barnes and Co., 1876, 65-66).

infinitely higher than our own. If you long for a spiritual breakthrough in your life, seek God for it, but be patient. Sometimes God has us wait, to refine our motives. Make sure you don't want more of the Spirit so you can join some class of spiritual elites or so you can find acceptance or respect among those whom you admire. Surrender any part of you that might want to "see your name in lights." Ambition for godly service is a wonderful thing as long as our heart's prayer is, "*Thine* is the kingdom and the power and the glory" and not "*Mine* is the kingdom and the power and the glory."

We can't see the deepest recesses of our own hearts. Thank God that He sees and still loves us. He knew everything about us before He called us to Himself. We can trust Him to work in us His highest, best, and most loving purpose for our lives. "For I know the plans I have for you," declares the LORD, "plans to prosper you and not to harm you, plans to give you hope and a future" (Jeremiah 29:11).

It may be possible, too, that God is working some kind of inner healing or victory in your life so that when the time of breakthrough does come, you will be able to maintain your gains. Before the Israelites entered the Promised Land, God disclosed to them that though the entire land was their possession, He would not let them take it all at once. Why not? I'm sure that had they had their way, they would have wanted their inheritance all at once. But God knew better. They were still too small a people for the expanse of land He was giving them. If they gained too much ground too quickly, the wild beasts would multiply against them and attack them on every path. He had a better plan. Instead, He would give it to them, "little by little," as they grew into it (see Exodus 23:28–30; Deuteronomy 7:22).

Similarly, in our spiritual lives, God may sometimes withhold spiritual breakthroughs or dimensions of the Spirit's working in and through us because we haven't yet "grown" spiritually in areas of character, Christian discipline, and general maturity where we can successfully handle it. We may be prone to being judgmental or spiritually proud. (I once had a friend who confessed that God could only use him once a month, that more than that gave him a big head! I hope that by now he has grown past that stage!) God does humble us for our own good.

Or, perhaps we need specific spiritual preparation before we experience the breakthroughs we are seeking. There could be an area or areas in our lives where God wants to cleanse or strengthen us before He entrusts more of His power and gifts to us. Being filled with the Spirit will certainly make us more of a threat to the devil, and we need to be fortified and ready for his attacks. Let's not forget the barrage of satanic temptations thrown at Jesus! This assault on Him immediately followed His baptism and the Holy Spirit's coming upon Him, and it immediately preceded His miracle-working, Holy Spirit-empowered ministry (see Matthew 3:11–4:10).

God could also be teaching us to walk by faith and not feelings, often a very hard lesson to learn. There may be many reasons He does what He does. God sometimes—and often for a purpose known only to Him — says to us, "Trust me in this. Wait." This shouldn't make us feel bad. Don't forget that with greater release of God's Spirit in our lives, there comes greater responsibility for service and greater accountability to God: "From everyone who has been given much, much will be demanded; and from the one who has been entrusted with much, much more will be asked" (Luke 12:48). This gives us no excuse for holding back from seeking and serving God, but it should give us peace as we wait on the Lord and use the talents He has already given us, whether they be one, five, or ten.

In closing this chapter, I want to share with you a very beautiful and powerful poem written as a dialogue between God and one of His beloved children who has become discouraged with waiting.

Child, You Must Wait!

Desperately, helplessly, longingly, I cried:
Quietly, patiently, lovingly God replied.
I pled and I wept for a clue to my fate,
and the Master so gently said, "Child, you must wait".

"Wait? You say, wait!" my indignant reply.
"Lord, I need answers, I need to know why!
Is your hand shortened? Or have you not heard?
By Faith, I have asked, and am claiming your Word.
My future and all to which I can relate
hangs in the balance, and YOU tell me to WAIT?

"I'm needing a 'yes', a go-ahead sign,
or even a 'no' to which I can resign.
And Lord, You promised that if we believe
we need but to ask, and we shall receive.
And Lord, I've been asking, and this is my cry:
I'm weary of asking! I need a reply!"
Then quietly, softly, I learned of my fate
as my Master replied once again, "You must wait."
So, I slumped in my chair, defeated and taut
and grumbled to God, "So, I'm waiting . . . for what?"

He seemed, then, to kneel, and His eyes wept with mine,
and he tenderly said, "I could give you a sign.
I could shake the heavens, and darken the sun.
I could raise the dead, and cause mountains to run.
All you seek, I could give, and pleased you would be.
You would have what you want—
but, you wouldn't know Me.

"You'd not know the depth of My love for each saint;
you'd not know the power that I give to the faint;
you'd not learn to see through the clouds of despair;
you'd not learn to trust just by knowing I'm there;
you'd not know the joy of resting in Me
when darkness and silence were all you could see."

"You'd never experience that fullness of love
as the peace of My Spirit descends like a dove;
you'd know that I give and I save . . . (for a start)
but you'd not know the depth of the beat of My heart.

"The glow of My comfort late into the night,
the faith that I give when you walk without sight,

the depth that's beyond getting just what you asked
of an infinite God, who makes what you have LAST.

"You'd never know, should your pain quickly flee,
what it means that 'My grace is sufficient for Thee.'
Yes, your dreams and desires overnight would come true,
but, oh, the loss, if I lost what I'm doing in you!"

—Author unknown

Chapter 4

What Does It Mean To Be "Spirit-Filled"?

When I think about what it means to be "Spirit-filled," two experiences from my past come to mind. First is the woman I wrote about in Scene 1 of this book's Introduction. As you might recall, she claimed her husband—although a drunken adulterer—was "Spirit-filled" and that she was not. And what was the standard by which she defined Spirit-filled? "He speaks in tongues, but I don't." It doesn't matter *what* tradition we may be part of, by *no* stretch of the imagination should that be considered an acceptable definition of what it means to be filled with God's Spirit.

I do understand how some people have come to believe that. In a number of passages in the book of Acts, most notably in Acts 2:1–4 and Acts 10:44–46, speaking in tongues did accompany the experience of being filled with the Holy Spirit. Certainly, the gift of tongues is a valid spiritual gift, and I believe it is beneficial, particularly as a prayer language for individual believers (see Chapter 6: "What About Speaking in Tongues?" and Chapter 7: "My Personal Experience with Tongues"). But many other Scriptures help define the true meaning of "Spirit-filled." These convince us that this woman's husband certainly was *not* filled with God's Spirit. *The Scriptures do not support the use of one spiritual gift to determine who is Spirit-filled and who is not.* I'm sure that few, if any, Pentecostals would ever say this woman's husband was truly Spirit-filled, but because of the way the phrase "Spirit-filled" is often used, there is cause for misunderstanding.

My second memory that relates to the meaning of being Spirit-filled comes from my experience and training with the little blue Holy Spirit booklet published and circulated by Bill Bright's Campus Crusade for Christ.[7] Bill Bright was a tremendous, world-changing Christian leader whom God used amazingly to mobilize and train millions of Christians to share their faith in Christ. Heaven will be populated, no doubt, with millions of people who came to Christ, from every nation and language, because of Bill Bright's incredible vision and anointing for leadership.

Millions of copies of this booklet have been distributed in most major languages around the world. I have found it to be very helpful in a number of respects:

- It encourages Christians to *move beyond regeneration and to seek God for an empowering* of the Holy Spirit for more effective Christian living and also—and very importantly—for sharing our faith in Christ with others.
- It provides a *solid biblical basis* for encouraging Christians to seek to be Spirit-filled. It points to God's *command* that we be filled with the Spirit, and also to the *assurance from God's Word*, that, if we pray according to God's will, He will answer our prayer. Since God commands us to be filled, we know it is His will, so we can expect Him to answer our prayer when we ask Him to fill us with the Holy Spirit.

God has used this booklet in my life and in the lives of multitudes of others who seek to be more Christ-like and more effective in our witness for Christ. I am sure it has accomplished what it was intended to do.

One thing, however, that the booklet does not do is to present a full understanding of the Spirit-filled life. Using our Holy Spirit Gift Box and packages analogy, this booklet encourages us to open *some* of the packages in the box but completely ignores other ones. Again, I am sure the booklet does accomplish what it was designed to do.

---

[7] You can read a copy of this booklet, "Have You Made the Wonderful Discovery of the Spirit-filled Life?" at http://spirit-filled-life.com/english/default.htm.

However, if we want a fuller understanding of what the Spirit-filled life is about, we must look elsewhere.

My reason for giving attention to the Campus Crusade Holy Spirit booklet, in particular, is that in many significant ways it represents the mainstream evangelical understanding of the Spirit-filled life. Generally speaking, mainstream evangelicals embrace regeneration, the fruit of the Spirit, koinonia/fellowship and power to witness. Ever-growing numbers now open the "Praise and Worship" package, as well. But when it comes to the package called "Spiritual Gifts," specifically under the subheading, "supernatural," there is often a pronounced silence at best, or an undermining through fear tactics, attempts to explain it all away, or even outright vilification. Some have allowed themselves to become tied up in theological straight-jackets, concluding—on *very* shaky biblical grounds—that "God no longer does those things" (more on this in Chapter 6). Others, having never been exposed to such things, don't see this package as even entering into their spiritual life equation. It remains wrapped, hidden, forgotten somewhere at the bottom of the box.

I contend that neither of the two uses of the word Spirit-filled presented above is adequate for answering our question, "What does it mean to be Spirit-filled?" Both understandings take *some* packages out of the Holy Spirit box but leave others wrapped up and ignored. In searching the Scriptures for what it means to be filled with the Spirit, I have discovered at least six characteristics clearly linked with the Spirit-filled life.

1. Spirit-filled Christians Demonstrate an Abiding State of Spiritual Growth and Christ-like Character

Those who are filled with the Holy Spirit are maturing spiritually, demonstrating a genuine love relationship with God and a Christ-like character. God's Spirit leads, empowers, and controls them as a general way of life.

In Acts 6:3, the apostles advised the newly formed church, "Brothers, choose seven men from among you who are *known to be full of the Spirit and of wisdom.*" The church needed leaders known for their integrity to carry out administrative leadership among the people. The ones they chose were recognizably filled with the Spirit, showing maturity and character, as well as giftedness.

In Acts 11:24, we see Barnabas, another leader, described as "a *good man, full of the Holy Spirit* and *faith.*" He, too, possessed a clearly recognizable Christ-like character. In Acts 4:36–37, we learn that his faithful walk in the Spirit and his great generosity had earned him his name "Barnabas," which means "son of encouragement."

In Acts 2:41-42, devotion to the things of God is a result of being filled with the Spirit. The believers devoted themselves to the apostles' teaching, to fellowship, and to prayer. They had an earnest desire to grow spiritually, to becoming spiritually wise and mature.

In Galatians 5:22, Paul describes the "the fruit of the Spirit" working in the lives of believers as "love, joy, peace, patience, kindness, goodness, faithfulness, gentleness, and self-control." As these qualities manifest in our lives, we see the character and personality of Jesus Christ. Those who are filled with the Holy Spirit become *Christ-like*!

I've heard that *a virtue is not a virtue until it has been tested.* When our son Billy Ford was a freshman at a prestigious southern California college, he played on the varsity water polo team. Before school even began the team went to San Diego for a tournament, and one night the team gathered around a campfire for the express purpose of bragging about their sexual exploits. Everyone participated, and the stories seemed to get worse as they went along. The last person called on to share was Billy. Since he was just starting to get acclimated to his new surroundings and wanted to be accepted, this situation was especially distressing for him. Nonetheless, when it came time for him to speak, he took a deep breath, prayed a silent prayer, and then said with genuine humility, "Well, frankly, I am a virgin. I have a girlfriend and everything, but I am a Christian, and I have decided to wait until I am married to have sex." The impact of those words on the rest of the team was considerable.

Billy continued to resist temptation, demonstrating genuine Christ-like character all the way through college and then seminary. It is not a surprise that he is now a dedicated pastor. He and wife Denise have served at Bouquet Canyon Church in Santa Clarita, CA for over five years now, and they have five precious children.

My friend, Joe Delahunt, is the Senior Pastor of Silliman Baptist Church in Bridgeport, Connecticut and the President of the American Baptist Churches of Connecticut. Following a renewal weekend at his church, his congregation was hit hard with news of serious health issues of several prominent members of their church. I realized that this church has real Christ-like character when Joe told me: "(As a result of the renewal in the Holy Spirit) . . . we are more aggressive in healing prayer, and we're growing in faith and courage. These assaults on our members have left us shell-shocked; but we have expectancy–even with grim problems–that God will do great things!"

Perseverance. Faithfulness. Christ-like character. Far too often, we relegate this facet of what it means to be Spirit-filled to a low place on the list of spiritual priorities. Some Christians and churches have such a hunger for powerful and dramatic manifestations that character issues get sidelined. I know firsthand of a church that quickly elevated a man to a central leadership position when they saw how gifted he was. This amazingly gifted man was an impressive Bible teacher who also operated dramatically in the gifts of the Spirit. With such an ability to wow a crowd, he soon had quite a following.

Then the day came when he made a shocking announcement to his fellow church leaders: He was divorcing his wife and marrying a woman whom he'd been counseling. When questioned, he conceded that he knew God "generally" was against divorce, but that He had granted an exception in his case. Of course, this sent the church reeling. Sadly, this man's charisma swayed some in the church. They actually supported his decision, convinced that God had given him a special dispensation. The lead pastor, however, held his ground against this man's behavior. Eventually the man left the church. They discovered *after he left* that he had done this same thing *five times* before! To top it off, he took his new wife to another well-known church some forty miles away and within a few months was in leadership there. The last I heard, he was married to his *seventh* wife!

Jesus said: "By their fruit you will recognize them . . . A good tree cannot bear bad fruit, and a bad tree cannot bear good fruit" (Matthew 7:16-18). If our lives bear bad fruit, we insult the Holy Spirit if we claim to be Spirit-filled. Too many Christian leaders, though endowed with tremendous spiritual gifts, lack the most basic and essential virtues of moral purity, financial integrity, and personal and professional accountability; consequently, they end up dragging Christ's name through the mud *for all the world to see*. Recent history is strewn with examples of this. The fallen leaders themselves aren't fully to blame, however. We Christians so often allow church culture to become so infected with the spirit and values of the world—materialism, thrill-seeking, power-trips, hero-worship—that such things are almost guaranteed to happen.

Many of our evangelical "subcultures" and churches allow "touch-not-the-Lord's-anointed" and "Moses-syndrome" concepts of leadership to intimidate them into quietly resigning themselves to the outrageous behavior of leaders. Please! The call to support our leaders does *not* mean that we silently watch while they spurn the blood of our Lord Jesus Christ and hold His Name and His church up for public contempt and ridicule. Leaders must be held accountable to exhibit Christian character by their fellow leaders, churches, and denominations. If they/we refuse accountability, then they/we should not be in the ministry. It is sad when the non-Christian world often has a better grasp on standards of behavior acceptable for Christian leadership than the leaders and members of Christ's body. Cheap grace and false mercy must be renounced and replaced by a genuine regard for the holiness, as well as the love, of God.

2. Spirit-filled Christians Are Motivated and Empowered to Share Their Faith with Others

Those who are filled with the Holy Spirit have received the *power* of the Spirit to proclaim the gospel of Jesus Christ. Prior to Pentecost in Acts 1:8, Jesus promised His disciples, "You will receive *power* when the Holy Spirit comes on you; and you will be *my witnesses* in Jerusalem, and in all Judea and Samaria, and to the ends of the earth." The word "power" used here is translated from the Greek word *dunamis*, from which we derive our words "dynamic" and "dynamite." The Holy Spirit anoints us with POWER to exalt Jesus Christ and to make Him known to others.

The Day of Pentecost saw the fulfillment of Christ's prediction, when Peter, now filled with the Holy Spirit, preached the gospel powerfully and boldly. In Acts 4:8, we see him "filled with the Holy Spirit" and preaching the gospel to Israel's leaders. In Acts 4:31, following a prayer meeting at which the disciples asked God for boldness and for the power of signs and wonders to accompany their preaching, we read, "the place where they were meeting was shaken. And they were all *filled with the Holy Spirit and spoke the Word of God boldly*."

A person who is Spirit-filled is a witness for Christ. Someone who never witnesses and has no passion for winning people to Jesus has no business describing himself as a "Spirit-filled" Christian.

I like the word *audacity*. This word means *fearless daring, bold, heedless of restraints*. Since the Holy Spirit gives us the *audacity* to witness effectively for Christ, let me propose to you that He is *The Divine Audacitator*.

The exciting thing about this is the great exhilaration and empowerment the Holy Spirit gives us *while* we are witnessing. We may not feel very powerful at the outset, but as we step out in faith, the Holy Spirit fills us, enabling us to rise to the occasion. We find ourselves saying things we didn't know we knew, and saying them in very persuasive and effective ways. Could this be because the Holy Spirit is a Person, and as a Person, He gets excited when we step out and share our faith? I believe so. I believe our obedience so delights and energizes Him that He leaps to action and fires us up.

One day the Holy Spirit leaped to action in my daughter Hannah's life. At the time she was a nineteen-year-old student at a university known as a hostile bastion of Christian-bashing. On this occasion she was in her drama class. Depicting an auto accident, students ran around as if panic-stricken, screaming all kinds of obscenities and using Jesus' name as an expletive. The director asked if the language offended anyone. Hannah spoke up: "I'd appreciate it if you wouldn't use Jesus' name that way," she said. Staring at her hard, he sneered and said mockingly for all to hear, "Well, what do we have here? Are you one of those *born-again Christians?"* Hannah looked him squarely in the eyes and spoke back with full confidence, "Totally!"

This one word so shook and unnerved this young man that he immediately backed off and resumed the play. The next day, he spotted Hannah on campus and came straight to her. "I've got to talk to you about your relationship with God," he said. After listening to him pour out his heart, Hannah shared her faith in Christ with him. She then put her hand on his shoulder and prayed for him for quite some time, right on the campus with other students walking by. It's hard to believe that Hannah was once a very shy young lady — shy, that is, until *The Divine Audacitator* took hold of her. Now, she sings the Lord's praises all over the world. For some amazing footage of a spontaneous outpouring of the Holy Spirit at Disneyland, visit www.youtube.com/hannahfordmusic!

In addition to sharing the gospel, this power to witness for Christ is demonstrated in many ways. The gospel can be proclaimed powerfully through music and singing, through dramas, and writing. When a group of Christians genuinely loves and praises God, when they show love for one another, when they demonstrate compassion for those in pain or in dire need, and when they make sacrifices for the One they love, these all can be Spirit-empowered witnesses for Christ. A clear fruit of the life of the Spirit-filled community described in Acts 2:41–47 is this: "And the Lord added to their number daily those who were being saved."

3. Spirit-filled Christians Receive Spiritual Gifts That May Come as an "Inspiration of the Moment."

Those who are filled with the Holy Spirit are willing and yielded vessels, ready for the Holy Spirit's use in supernatural ways for particular situations. The Holy Spirit comes upon these people, enabling them to be His instruments for accomplishing God's will.

In Acts 13:4–12, we find Paul and Barnabas in a town called Paphos on the island of Cyprus. A Jewish sorcerer named Bar-Jesus (or Elymas) opposed them as they shared Christ with a town leader who had keen interest in the message. Fed up with this interference, "Paul, *filled with the Holy Spirit*, looked straight at Elymas and said, 'You are a child of the devil . . . Now the hand of the Lord is against you. You are going to be blind, and for a time you will be unable to see the light of the sun.'" Immediately, the man was struck blind and had to grope his way along, looking for someone to lead him. The amazed leader instantly became a believer.

In this situation, and in many others recorded in the book of Acts, the Holy Spirit enabled Christ's ministers to rise to the occasion and deal with demonic opposition (as here and in Acts 16:16–19), disease and physical afflictions (as in Acts 3, where God used Peter to heal the lame man), and in many other situations. We read so many accounts of these supernatural manifestations in the Book of Acts that it seems quite the normal occurrence.

Many of the spiritual gifts operate like this (see 1 Corinthians 12:4–7), as "inspirations of the moment." If we are filled with the Holy Spirit, He can use us in unexpected supernatural ways to meet people's deepest needs. He can use us in the area of healing, or in sharing with people words of knowledge or words of wisdom from Him to help and encourage them. He can speak a prophetic message through us for a certain person or within a fellowship meeting or worship service that can touch and stir hearts. One story of healing comes from Rev. Les Cantrell, Pastor of First Baptist Church in McPherson Kansas, home to over 300 worshipers. This healing occurred at their 2009 Youth Summer Camp:

> One of the kids on the fringes of the group had a bad back and wanted to go home. Anna Lutke, our retreat speaker, and a group of friends, prayed for him, and he was instantaneously healed. Our youth workers began to embrace learning how to pray for healing, and their expectancy was greatly increased. The next week one of the youth was injured while playing Frisbee. The ER attending physician said he had a broken clavicle. The entire youth group gathered around and laid hands on him as they prayed for healing, after which further x-rays showed that he had no broken bones. The kid was back playing football in two weeks! Our faith and expectancy are growing immensely!

Of course, many spiritual gifts are not generally so spontaneous in their use; for example, administration, leadership, acts of mercy, generous giving, hospitality, and teaching. But they, too, by virtue of the fact that they are not just natural abilities but are Spirit-given and Spirit-anointed enablements, can give us the ability to respond to needs and circumstances far more spontaneously, powerfully, and effectively than we can with our own natural abilities. (See Number 4 below for discussion of spiritual gifts as they relate more specifically to building up the body of Christ.)

This area of the spontaneous and supernatural scares some of us. We like the safety of being people of "the Book" (and rightly so). Of course, the Word of God is and always must be our highest authority; spiritual experiences cannot take precedence over the Scriptures. Naturally, the authority of God's Word should be non-negotiable to us. The problem is this: *that very Word of God introduces us to these supernatural gifts, validates them, and encourages us to seek them!*

Paul urges us in 1 Corinthians 14:1 to "Follow the way of love and *eagerly desire the spiritual gifts*, especially the gift of prophecy" (which, we must admit if we're really honest with the testimonies of scripture, is more than simply anointed preaching).

Far from departing from God's Word, it is precisely *because* we are people of "the Book" that we must open ourselves to what the Spirit did in the early church and what He can to do today if we stop blocking Him. We in *no* way betray the authority of the Bible when we appropriate the blessings, power, and gifts of the Spirit. The Bible urges us to desire them—*eagerly*! Danger only comes with the extremes: First, when we value supernatural manifestations so highly that we no longer care whether or not they are founded on Scripture, or whether we use them according to Scriptural parameters. Second, when we resist the Spirit by keeping Him "in the box," relegating His activity to distant history rather than present day experience.

Granted, there are some wild and crazy things done in the name of the Holy Spirit. But, to use an overworked idiom, *we must not throw the baby out with the bathwater*. Our concerns about unbalanced teachings and excessive practices by some must never cause us to stiff-arm the entire supernatural realm of the Holy Spirit's gifts and manifestations. Let's not forget that "the Kingdom of God is not a matter of talk but of *power*" (1 Corinthians 4:20). Paul considered the "power of signs and miracles, through the power of the Spirit" to be an essential part of the full proclamation of the gospel. (Romans 15:18–19).

Often it was the demonstration of the Spirit's power that got the attention of the crowds and drew them to hear and respond to the gospel of Christ. Take for example Paul's and Barnabus' ministry in Iconium (Acts 14:1–7) where the Lord "confirmed the message of His grace by enabling them to do miraculous signs and wonders" (14:3). Or, in Ephesus, where "God did extraordinary miracles through Paul" (Acts 19:11); and where, in the name of Jesus, he "outgunned" the sons of Sceva in the ministry of casting out demons; and where sinners were seized with fear, and the name of Jesus was held in "high honor," resulting in a revival and the public burning of occult literature (19:13–20). Wow! Can anyone say we don't need this today?

The Lord used Peter in Acts 9:32–35 to heal a paralytic who had been in bed for eight years. The result: "*All those who lived in Lydda and Sharon saw him and turned to the Lord.*" Again, in Acts 9:36–42 we read of how God used Peter to raise Tabitha from the dead. The result: "*many people believed in the Lord*" (v. 42). Wouldn't it be wonderful if all those living in Los Angeles, New Orleans, Dallas, or wherever, saw the wonders of God and turned to the Lord?

Indeed, in our day, there are numerous stories of miracles and healings taking place around us. As a result, many come to faith in Christ. Missionaries doing pioneer work among spiritually pagan people groups report amazing signs and wonders done in the name of Jesus, resulting in numerous conversions to Christ.[8] God is using Heidi and Roland Baker (Iris Ministries) to do astounding miracles of healings and conversions in Mozambique, Africa, where the compassion and healing power of Jesus seem straight out of the Gospels or the Book of Acts. Here in the United States, Randy Clark of Global Awakening, Bill Johnson at Bethel Church in Redding, California and many others have developed a culture of faith for miracles. They are also traveling extensively and writing books, lifting the faith and opening the eyes of hundreds of thousands if not millions all over the world. Randy Clark's new book, *There Is More: Reclaiming the Power of Impartation*, is very helpful in many ways. A fascinating documentary film entitled *The Finger of God* (2007), produced by Darren Wilson, is a great resource for finding out what is happening in different parts of the world; Darren's new release, *Furious Love* (2010), is also very powerful and eye-opening.

A growing number of Baptists, too, are getting in on this focus and move of God. Dr. John Piippo is the Senior Pastor of Redeemer

---

[8] For example, these two books by Jane Rumph: *Signs and Wonders in America Today: Amazing Accounts of God's Power*, Vine Books, 2003, and *Stories from the Front Lines: Power Evangelism in Today's World*, Chosen Books, 1996.

Fellowship Church, an American Baptist church in Monroe, Michigan, the home of 350-400 on-fire Christians who pray for miracles and see many happen. One woman whose body was riddled with cancerous tumors was completely healed. In addition to being a pastor, John is also a professor at both college and seminary levels. He mentors doctoral students for Palmer Seminary in Philadelphia, and his church now has started the Redeemer School of Ministry, where students are growing in faith and anointing. "People need *God*," John says, "not humans. Clear the way! Come, Holy Spirit!"

Rev. Clint Webb is the Senior Pastor at Church on the Rock in Oak Harbor, Washington and also the mentor pastor for pastors in the American Baptist Churches of the Northwest. COTR has several hundred members, with lots of turnover due to their location beside a naval base. They see multitudes of people coming to Jesus every year, with scores of baptisms. They also pray for miracles and see many happen. One Navy officer was healed after prayer; his heart had stopped and there was no brain activity, but God raised him up! Another man was brought to the church in a wheelchair with encephalitis of the brain. He was healed and came back to tell everyone about it. "I'm not boasting," Clint said, "The *Holy Spirit* is doing it!"

The Rev. Keith Cerk is the Pastor of First Baptist Church of Waukegan, Illinois. He once met a homeless man who hadn't eaten for two days because of a painful infection in his mouth. Keith prayed for him, and he was completely healed. The next Sunday the homeless man brought two other homeless friends to church. "God is near, He's present, He cares," Keith says; "When God heals like this, He charges everybody's faith."

In my own ministry, I was asked to go into an ICU to pray for a forty-eight year old friend of a son of one of my church friends. "He is not a Christian," my friend said, "and he may not let us pray for him. But doctors are calling in all the relatives, because his organs are shutting down and he may not last the day." We asked God to activate the organs, and then led the man in prayer to receive Christ. I received word later that day that the man's organs had suddenly activated, and the man went home well two days later. There are no doubt hundreds, even thousands of such miracles happening every day all across our country and throughout the world.

Frankly, I don't understand the reasoning of some who believe and teach that "these things don't happen any more" when there is so much evidence to the contrary. Obviously, the need for God's power is just as pronounced in our world today as it was in the first century. Multitudes of desperately needy people are all around us. Most are lost, confused, entangled in sins, and shaped by intellectual and spiritual forces that are hostile to Jesus Christ. Pagan religions and demonically empowered occult practices continue to proliferate. In this battle for souls, should we content ourselves with presenting cerebral doctrinal formulations of the gospel from spiritually anemic churches? Will that impress this generation? *Of course not!* Why would we content ourselves with powerlessness when the Holy Spirit can confirm our message with signs and wonders?

The powers of darkness are on the march, and they have a full arsenal for keeping the world in their pocket. In the face of such encroaching evil, trying to justify powerlessness is inexcusable. We must *want* the power of God; and we must *cry out* for it: ***"Thy Kingdom come, Thy will be done, on earth as it is in heaven!"*** The Biblical case for disbelieving in the modern day validity of the supernatural gifts, such as those recorded in Acts and in 1 Corinthians 12–14, is woefully unconvincing. At this crucial time in world history, not only is it unwise, it is downright *dangerous* to put the Holy Spirit in a theological straight-jacket. Sadly, by leaving the "signs and wonders" portion of our spiritual gifts package wrapped and left in the Holy Spirit Gift Box, we actually hinder the fulfillment of Christ's Great Commission.

4. Spirit-filled Christians Fully Participate in Christ-Centered Fellowship and Body Life

Those who are filled with the Holy Spirit are not "lone rangers" whose total Christian experience is vertical—"me and Jesus." After committing themselves to Christ, they also commit themselves horizontally as they find their place in the body of Christ.

The apostle Peter describes this twofold conversion process of first coming to Christ and then participating in Christ's body: "As you come to Him, the living Stone . . . you also, like living stones, are being built into a spiritual house to be a holy priesthood, offering spiritual sacrifices acceptable to God through Jesus Christ" (1 Peter 2:4-5). The Christian life is not a superficial gathering together of isolated individual believers. When the Holy Spirit came upon the early Christians, they were together with one heart and soul. In Acts 2:41–47 we see just how much they were together: "All the believers were *together* and had everything in common . . . every day they continued to meet *together* . . . they broke bread in their homes and ate *together* with glad and sincere hearts."

In addition to boldness for preaching (previously discussed), there was another result of the believers being filled with the Holy Spirit: "All the believers were one in heart and mind. No one claimed that any of his possessions was his own, but they shared everything in common" (Acts 4:31-32). Out of this coming together, the Holy Spirit makes us into a family. He gives each of us spiritual gifts, and He motivates us to use those gifts to build up the church (see 1 Peter 4:10). Pastor Jon Good, the sharp young Pastor of Covenant Baptist Church in West Bloomfield, Michigan, says:

> The greatest work of the Holy Spirit in our church is *UNITY*. Our church is multiracial and multi-cultural, and multi-generational. From worship styles to putting meals together in the kitchen, there are lots of stories–relationships, daily dealing with each other–where the Holy Spirit has brought us together in unity. He brings about a willingness of the human spirit, a sof-

> tening of walls that separate; He enables us to listen, to build relationships, to learn about each other and grow in our understanding. We are becoming more open and honest, more real. You can't hide and expect God to do something.

There is power when we participate in genuine Spirit-filled Christian fellowship. Jesus said, "For where two or three of you come together in my name, there am I with them" (Matthew 18:20). Of course, Jesus lives in us as individuals and He is with us all the time. But the Holy Spirit adds another dimension of His presence and power when we gather together in His name.

I will never forget a special personal experience that made me appreciate this truth in new ways. When our children were still young, Cheri and I took them to Disneyland. Since I had been a youth pastor in Southern California for a number of years, I had been to Disneyland numerous times and was not at all excited about being there again. The weather was dreary and overcast, I had grudgingly spent a lot of money on admission tickets, and I just plain didn't want to be there. In fact, I felt somewhat depressed and irritable. Had I been a Disney character that day, my name would have been "Grumpy."

Once inside the park, my children spotted "Goofy," the dog in many Disney cartoons. They ran to him, eager to shake his hand. Obviously, Goofy was a person dressed up in an elaborate costume with a huge happy mask that entirely covered his head. He was thoroughly enjoying himself as he danced around and shook hands with all who came up to him. I meandered over to him, following my kids, and I started to put my hand out to shake his. As he extended his hand toward me, something very remarkable happened. Our hands never met. Instead, without any thought of doing so, our arms reached out toward one another and we found ourselves embracing in a warm bear hug. Amazingly, I experienced the very powerful presence of the Holy Spirit, and I said to him (or her), "You are a Christian, aren't you?"

Without saying a word—masked Disney characters aren't allowed to speak—he took Cheri's hand and "drew" on her palm with his finger the shape of a cross. Then he used his finger to write the letters "B-O-R-N A-G-A-I-N." I tingled all over! A fellow Christian, whose face I could not even see, from whom I heard no voice or words, had brightened my whole day. The Holy Spirit in him and the Holy Spirit in me drew us together in a way that lifted me up and gave me a joyous heart for the rest of the day.

That experience still amazes me because I had no visible or audible cues that told me "Goofy" was a Christian. It was purely and simply the presence of the Holy Spirit that revealed it to me. Think about this: If that one encounter with one fellow Christian whom I didn't even know was a Christian had so much power to bless and strengthen and encourage me, imagine how much blessing, strengthening and encouragement comes to us when we deliberately come together with brothers and sisters in Christ to worship Him, pray together, study His Word, and serve Him as a team.

It would be extremely difficult to overemphasize the importance of fellowship for Christ-centered, Spirit-filled living. The spiritual gifts of healing, words of knowledge, prophecy, words of encouragement, and others generally are released within the context of the body gathered together.

In one small group Cheri and I belonged to, the Holy Spirit used our prayers for one another dramatically to heal two of our men. One was on medical leave from his job, suffering from an emotional breakdown; the other had been diagnosed by his doctor to have five or six things wrong with him. The man experiencing the emotional crisis was completely healed. The amazed doctor sent him back to work the next week. The other man was healed of all but one of his conditions, and that one was greatly improved.

When we are filled with the Holy Spirit, He knits our hearts together as one; He gives us abilities that He enables us to use (see 1 Corinthians 12 and Romans 12), and He coordinates our activities to build up Christ's body. A healthy body of believers produces mature and healthy Christians (see Ephesians 4:11–16). Our participation in Christ-centered, Spirit-filled community is God's primary plan for bringing us to spiritual maturity. If you *are* Spirit-filled, you *will be* motivated to be in fellowship; and if you *want* to be Spirit-filled, you *must* be in fellowship.

I leave this section with one passage of Scripture — Act 14:19–20 — that speaks for itself: "They stoned Paul and dragged him out of the city, thinking he was dead. But *after the disciples had gathered around him*, he got up and went back into the city." Praise the Lord!

5. Spirit-filled Christians Praise and Worship God

A person who is filled with the Holy Spirit is a *worshiper*! In Ephesians 5:18–20, Paul says this about the Spirit-filled life:

> Do not get drunk on wine which leads to debauchery. Instead, *be filled with the Spirit.* Speak to one another with psalms, hymns, and spiritual songs. Sing and make music in your heart to the Lord, always giving thanks to God the Father in the name of our Lord Jesus Christ.

Acts 2:46–47 describes the early church as having "glad and sincere hearts" and as "praising God."

In the late sixties and early seventies, when I was a new Christian, the primary focus of the evangelical church seemed to be *personal evangelism.* Campus Crusade for Christ trained thousands to share the "Four Spiritual Laws," and James Kennedy launched his "Evangelism Explosion" from Ft. Lauderdale, Florida. I was well trained in both methods and still can recite the main points of each.

In the mid-seventies through the early eighties, the primary focus became *body life*. Ray Stedman wrote the book *Body Life*, which became an "Exhibit A" of how the church was meant to function. Howard Snyder's two books, **The Problem of Wineskins** and **The Community of the King**[9] provided an exciting theological frame-

[9] The former has been republished as *Radical Renewal: The Problem of Wineskins Today* (Eugene, OR: Wipf and Stock Publishers, 2005. See also *The Community of the King*, revised edition (Downers Grove, IL: InterVarsity Press 2004).

work for this new thrust. Evangelism and its counterpart, social action, could not be effective if they were two arms reaching out from nothing. In order to reach people and effectively disciple them, there *must* be a body, a community, a family of believers, where new believers can find loving support and a place to put their gifts and abilities to good use in God's service.

A primary focus in the early to mid eighties on through the nineties, and certainly to the present day, has been what A.W. Tozer called "the missing jewel of the church": *worship*. Actually, the worship focus began earlier than the eighties but it took until the eighties to become part of mainstream evangelicalism. The move of God's Spirit beginning in the late sixties and early seventies, which encompassed the Jesus Movement and the Charismatic Movement, brought with it a gushing fountain of joyous and moving praise and worship songs. A spirit of worship—an awareness of the worthiness of God to be praised, worshiped, adored, honored, and glorified—has been sweeping the Christian world ever since. The Holy Spirit has inspired thousands of choruses which God has been using to move His church into ever-deepening dimensions of praise and worship. Many of the traditional hymns and choral anthems have not lost their place in worship, either. This explosive growth has brought worship music front and center in the life of the church. Some even call this resurgence of worship, "The Great Worship Awakening."

How exciting it is to see God's people come together in our day, often across denominational and cultural lines, to worship and praise God. God used me a number of years ago to start HEAL (**H**umboldt **E**vangelical **Al**liance), a network of evangelical churches in Humboldt County, California. HEAL included Southern Baptists, American Baptists, Foursquare, Assemblies of God, Nazarenes, non-denominational charismatics, Evangelical Free, Wesleyans, Congregationalists, Presbyterians and more. We periodically had joint prayer and praise rallies which were tremendously exhilarating as we came together to celebrate our unity in Christ and to worship our Lord.

God is moving by His Spirit to show us how to worship! Singing, music, a great variety of instruments, dance, banners, flags, marches, pageants, dramas—the Holy Spirit is *infinitely* creative, and I'm sure we've just scratched the surface of the wonder and glory to be found in worship.

We've come a long way from the era when "two hymns and special music" were seen primarily as a buildup to what was once viewed as the main feature of the service—the sermon. Of course, the sermon *is* an important time when God speaks to us through the preaching of His Word. But worship is a time where we enjoy a two-way communication with our God—when we can respond to Him, expressing our love and adoration directly to Him.

It now seems funny to me that what we used to call "worship services" consisted of so little true "worship." We would sing *about* God, testify *about* His goodness, tell others *about* Him, and try to bring others to faith in Him. But often we failed to offer anything directly *to* Him, except perhaps a pastoral prayer for *our* needs.

A glorious shift is taking place in our worship culture. In addition to all the other things we used to do, we now recognize that God *longs* for us to focus our attention and love directly *to Him*. No longer a prelude to what really matters, we sing our praises to adore *Him*, to express our love back to our wonderful God ("*God of wonders beyond our galaxy, You are holy, holy . . .*" or "*I'm coming back to the heart of worship, and it's all about you, it's all about you, Jesus*").[10] This new recognition of getting back to "the heart of worship" is certainly God-breathed. Worshiping our awesome God most certainly is a worthwhile goal, a primary focus, and an end in itself—whether or not we ever get to hear the sermon!

Think how our Heavenly Father feels when we enter His presence, not to make requests or demands, but just to let Him know how

---

[10] Steve Hindalong and Marc Byrd, "God of Wonders," New Spring Publishing, Inc., Storm Boy Music, Meaux Mercy, 2000; and Matt Redman, "Heart of Worship, Worship Together," Kingsway's Thankyou Music, 1999.

much we love and appreciate Him. Jesus said, "A time is coming and has now come when the *true worshipers will worship the Father in spirit and truth, for they are the kind of worshipers the Father seeks*" (John 4:23). Our Father *loves* us. He created us for fellowship with Himself, to be His beloved children. "He destined us for adoption as his children through Jesus Christ, according to the good pleasure of his will" (Ephesians 1:5, NRSV). "How *great* is the love the Father has lavished on us, that we should be called children of God!" (1 John 3:1). Our Heavenly Father *seeks* us, yearns for fellowship with us, invites us into His "holy of holies" and up into his "lap."

Our response is worship. It begins by offering ourselves fully to Him in surrender and service (see Romans 12:1), and also includes giving our praises and our offerings to Him (see Hebrews 13:15–16; 2 Corinthians 9:6–15). The apostle John takes us into the very heart of heaven in the book of Revelation, where we see what real worship is all about. Try to picture this:

> In a loud voice they sang: "Worthy is the Lamb, who was slain, to receive power and wealth and wisdom and strength and honor and glory and praise!" (Revelation 5:12).
>
> Then I heard every creature in heaven and on earth and under the earth and on the sea, and all that is in them, singing: "To Him who sits on the throne and to the Lamb be praise and honor and glory and power forever and ever!" The four living creatures said "Amen," and the elders fell down and worshiped (Revelation 5:13–14).
>
> After this I looked and there before me was a great multitude that no one could count, from every nation, tribe, people and language, standing before the throne and in front of the Lamb. They were wearing white robes and were holding palm branches in their hands. And they cried out in a loud voice: "Salvation belongs to our God, who sits on the throne, and to the Lamb" (Revelation 7:9–10).

> The twenty-four elders and the four living creatures fell down and worshiped God, who was seated on the throne. And they cried: "Amen, Hallelujah!" (Revelation 19:4).

When we pray the Lord's prayer, saying to God, *"Thy kingdom come, Thy will be done on earth as it is in heaven,"* we are in large measure praying that *the worship of God and His Son, Jesus Christ,* which is so central to the lifestyle of heaven, will be duplicated *here on the earth!* One of the Holy Spirit's roles is to bring this about. Oh, that we would all cry with the Psalmist, "Praise be to his glorious name forever; may the whole earth be filled with his glory. Amen and Amen" (Psalm 72:19).

A Spirit-filled Christian is a *worshiper.* Worship awakens a sense of *EXPECTANCY*, and sense of *WONDER!* My friend Paul Albrecht, Senior Pastor of the Journey Church in Westfield, Indiana says this: "The most dramatic role of the Holy Spirit is *atmosphere* in the church . . . Within that atmosphere, the Spirit touches people; we see it and call it for what it is–"this is a *Holy Spirit event.*" We come into worship prepared, but we aren't slaves to the worship format; we are open and expectant. He gives us a sense of *joyous expectancy!"*

Dr. Charles Revis, Executive Minister of the American Baptist Churches of the Northwest agrees: "The Holy Spirit enables worship that has a power, a presence to it, not just going through the motions. He brings a sense of excitement, a freedom for spontaneity in following His leading to pray for healing of bodies, relationships, hearts." Dr. John Piippo points to the same thing when he says, "Our services have no formal endings; they are not formulaic. There's expectancy! *Who knows what's going to happen?"*

Expectancy! Excitement! Wonder! God is alive—and He is worthy to be worshiped! Spirit-filled worshipers are not all alike in terms of their exuberance or outward displays of emotion and physical expression. For some, tapping a toe inside their shoe may be the outward expression of their hearty worship; others seem to want to do cartwheels down the aisle. We shouldn't try to coerce people, or ourselves, into expressiveness that isn't really sincere or genuine. On the other hand, neither should we try to impede ourselves or others from what is the genuine expression of our praise.

Our churches need to offer freedom for people to be the unique persons God has made us to be. We need mutual sensitivity, respect and tolerance for one another in areas where we differ. Where love reigns, our worship will bring blessing to God and also to us. Genuine worship is sincere, from the heart. In that regard, all who are filled with the Spirit will be the same.

We would all do well to remember: Worship is not about what *we* want or like or prefer. Worship is *for an audience of One!* Worship is for *God!* And He is *worthy*!

6. Spirit-filled Christians Have a Growing Compassion and Anointing to Minister to Other People

Those who are filled with the Holy Spirit will be moved by Christ's compassion and empowered by the Spirit to minister to the needs of other people. I recognize that there is some overlap here, particularly with Numbers 3 and 4, where spiritual gifts are also discussed. But each has a different focus.

Number 3's focus is the enabling of the Spirit that comes as an "inspiration of the moment." A Spirit-filled believer stands ready to be an instrument through whom the Holy Spirit can move spontaneously and supernaturally in a variety of circumstances. The emphasis is on inspired spontaneity and the supernatural dimension.

Number 4's focus is the Spirit's role in producing and maintaining true fellowship and body life. The Holy Spirit knits us into God's family and motivates us to use the spiritual gifts and abilities He gives us for building up the church.

In this next characteristic of the Spirit-filled life, the emphasis is on Holy Spirit inspired *compassion that equips and moves us to minister to the deepest needs of people*. Perhaps we can view it as the culmination of all the other characteristics, because it necessitates the character of Christ; the boldness and power to step out in faith as a witness; the availability to be used supernaturally and spontaneously, as circumstances require; and the power of the "two-or-three-gathered" team ministry. And it all grows out of a deep reverential and loving worship of God and the desire to please Him. "This is *to my Father's glory*," Jesus said, "that you bear much fruit, showing yourselves to be my disciples" (John 15:8). This characteristic ties the others together and reveals in the deepest way who Jesus Christ is and what He is about. Just listen to Jesus as He reads from Isaiah 61:1–2:

> The Spirit of the Lord is on me, because he has anointed me to preach good news to the poor. He has sent me to proclaim freedom for the prisoners and recovery of sight for the blind, to release the oppressed, to proclaim the year of the Lord's favor. (Luke 4:18–19)

After reading this, He then tells His hearers, "Today this scripture is fulfilled in your hearing."

Jesus was the "Christ," which means "the Anointed One" of God. He was anointed by the Spirit of God to proclaim good news, to set captives free, and give sight to the blind. Peter, preaching in the home of Cornelius, said: "You know what has happened throughout Judea . . . how God anointed Jesus of Nazareth with the Holy Spirit and power, and how He went around doing good and healing all who were under the power of the devil, because God was with Him" (Acts 10:37–38).

We see the fruit of this anointing for ministry throughout His earthly ministry, as multitudes were saved, healed, delivered, restored, blessed, raised from death to life, forgiven . . . and more. *Compassion* moved the heart of Jesus as He saw the desperately needy people around Him. His half-brother James testified of Him, "The Lord is full of *compassion* and mercy" (James 5:11). God's Word also says of Him, "When he saw the crowds, He had *compassion* on them, because they were harassed and helpless, like sheep without a shepherd" (Matthew 9:36). When large crowds came to see

Him and hear His teaching, "He had *compassion* on them and healed their sick" (Matthew 14:14). His *compassion* led Him to miraculously feed thousands of people (Matthew 15:32ff); heal the blind (Matthew 20:34); cure lepers (Mark 1:40–42). *Compassion* compelled Jesus to minister to people's deepest needs. It was *compassion* that drove Him to raise Lazarus from the dead, and the son of the widow from Nain. Jesus busted up every funeral He came across in the gospels!

My good friend Ray Schooler is the Director of Development and Church Relations for ABC-USA's International Ministries. He said, "There are about thirty-five miracles that Jesus performed recorded in Scripture. Of these, seven of them have to do with the power of Christ (turning water to wine, walking on water, etc.). But the other twenty-eight of the recorded miracles have to do with the *COMPASSION* of Jesus (feeding the hungry, healing the sick, forgiving sin, etc). Clearly we see the heart of God is compassion for hurting people!"

Finally, *compassion* led Jesus to the Cross of Calvary, where "God made him who had no sin to be sin for us," so that we could find reconciliation and peace with God, forgiveness of sins, restoration for our souls, deliverance from satanic deception and bondage, and everlasting life. In His *compassion*, He is like His Father, who so loved the world that He gave His only Son for us. Thank you, Lord! "Because of the Lord's great love we are not consumed, for his *compassions never fail*" (Lamentations 3:22).

But it doesn't end there. Jesus very clearly commissioned us—His disciples—to continue His mission. Of course, He alone is God the Son; we are not divine. And He alone was the Lamb of God, who died on the cross for the sins of the world. And only He is the mediator between the holy God and a fallen humanity: "For there is one God; there is also one mediator between God and humankind, Christ Jesus, himself human, who gave himself a ransom for all—this was attested at the right time"(1 Timothy 2:5–6, NRSV). Through His death and resurrection, Christ was not only the anointed Proclaimer of good news—He *is* the Good News!

He commissions *us* to be bearers of His message and instruments of His mission. In John 20:21–22, following His resurrection from the dead Jesus instructs His disciples, "*As the Father has sent me, I am sending you.*" He charged them to carry on His mission; He had the anointing to preach the good news, heal the brokenhearted, and set the captives free. Now, having made full salvation possible through the shedding of His blood and His resurrection from the dead, He commissioned His followers to preach the good news and to demonstrate its benefits, healing the sick and brokenhearted, setting captives free from the power of sin and Satan. Following this commissioning, "He breathed on them and said '*Receive the Holy Spirit*'" (v. 22).

When we are filled with the Holy Spirit, we are moved with the compassion of Jesus for people — people who are lost and lonely, sheep without a shepherd; people who are destitute, in body and in spirit; people who are bound by addictions and bent on self destruction; people so desperate for love that they sell their souls for acceptance and a sense of belonging. There are *so many* needy people everywhere, all around us, who need to know Jesus. They need His love, His restoring and healing power. They need His grace and forgiveness; His truth and meaning to bring clarity and purpose to their lives; His power to help them cope with life's problems and the hope that He alone can give. We need to get this. Our daughter Hannah is a Christian singer and songwriter. The first song she ever wrote, "Eyes of Compassion," came out of a vision she had where she saw the eyes of Jesus full of tears of compassion for people.

The Holy Spirit not only moves our hearts with the compassion of Jesus, He also moves us to act out of that compassion. He *anoints* us and *equips* us to minister to the deep needs of people. Sometimes we can do this as individuals, but He often leads us to minister to others as a team—as two or three gathered in His Name. The Holy Spirit moves us in compassion and makes us vessels through whom Jesus can carry on His ministry. We become His *voice* through which He speaks His words of truth and encouragement; His *hands* with which

He touches the lonely, the lost, and the "lepers" of our day; and His *feet*, which enable Him to go to those who need Him, whether that means across the street or in the remotest village on the other side of the world. Most of the missionaries associated with International Ministries exemplify this compassion of Jesus to an extraordinary extent. One example is the Night Light outreach in Bangkok, Thailand, where Annie Dieselberg and others reach out and rescue woman and children trapped in the sex trafficking trade, providing love, new life in Christ, jobs, deliverance, and discipleship.

The Isaiah 61:1–2 passage that Jesus cited is descriptive, not only of Jesus' ministry, but of ours, as well. The text continues beyond what Jesus quoted.

> "The Spirit of the Sovereign Lord is on me,
> because the Lord has anointed me . . .
> to comfort all who mourn,
>   and provide for those who grieve in Zion—
> to bestow on them a crown of beauty
>   instead of ashes,
> the oil of gladness
>   instead of mourning
> and a garment of praise
>   instead of a spirit of despair.
> They will be called oaks of righteousness,
>   a planting of the LORD
>   for the display of his splendor.
>
> Isaiah 61:1-3

The Holy Spirit gives this "Isaiah 61 Anointing" to us for the purpose of restoring people's lives, of bringing them into wholeness and strength, like "oaks of righteousness." Our deepest motivation in exercising this ministry is "for the display of His splendor," or as the American Standard Version puts it, *"that he may be glorified."*

Conclusion

In summary, we have found in the New Testament six major characteristics of the Spirit-filled life:

First, Spirit-filled Christians demonstrate an abiding state of spiritual growth and Christ-like character. Second, Spirit-filled Christians are motivated and empowered to share their faith in Christ with others. Third, Spirit-filled Christians are used as instruments of spiritual gifts that can come as an "inspiration of the moment." Fourth, Spirit-filled Christians fully participate in Christ-centered fellowship and body life. Fifth, Spirit-filled Christians are inspired to praise and worship God. And sixth, Spirit-filled Christians have a growing compassion and anointing to minister to other people.

I think it becomes clear as we observe these characteristics, that many of us have used the phrase "Spirit-filled" rather carelessly and without sufficient understanding as to the breadth and depth of its meaning. I would not presume to suggest in any way that you take my presentation of what it means to be Spirit-filled as final or definitive. I am sure that there are those who can to do a better job deducing and explaining these things. Nevertheless, I do believe the insights I have presented are close enough to the truth that we can all see this: When we talk about being "Spirit-filled," we need to do so with greater care and with deeper humility.

Spiritual pride is a killer. Not only does it lead to spiritual destruction in the lives of individual Christians, it also destroys unity in the Body of Christ. In matters dealing with the fullness of the Holy Spirit, we should seek to avoid terminology or inferences that tell other sincere believers in Christ that we believe *we* are Spirit-filled but that *they* are not. Our general human tendency is to judge others in areas where we show strength and to ignore areas where we show weakness. Let's avoid the pitfalls of personal and ecclesiastical self-aggrandizement and acknowledge that, though grateful for what God is already doing in us and through us, *all* of us still have a ways to go.

Some years ago, God spoke to me in a powerful way that made me weep and tremble. He had made me a leader, a pastor of a large church relative to the size of the county. Our church had significant ministries, including ones to the university campus and a very successful missions program that sent people to many nations of the world. He had also used me as a leader in county-wide events. I had become well-known in the Christian community and influential in many ways. I felt happy and pretty satisfied with myself . . . until God sent me a thunderbolt from His Word:

> Don't you know that you yourselves are God's temple and that God's Spirit lives in you? If anyone destroys God's temple, God will destroy him; for God's temple is sacred, and you are that temple. (1 Corinthians 3:16–17)

The context of this passage has to do with problems of pride and division in the church. The Corinthian church had tended toward divisiveness because of an overemphasis on the importance of individual Christian leaders and their teachings rather than on elevating Christ and centering their fellowship in Him. So God warned the Corinthians through Paul—and He warns us today—that the church is the temple of God's Spirit, that He considers it sacred and takes its health and welfare seriously. Those who destroy God's temple, God will destroy.

This scripture sent shivers down my spine as I recognized, in a deeper way than ever before, the depth of God's concern for the unity, health, and fruitfulness of Christ's body, the church. I understood acutely how crucial it is for me, as a leader, to use my ability, energy, and influence to build up Christ's body and promote the unity of the Holy Spirit (Ephesians 4:3), not just in my own church, but also in the larger body of Christ.

I felt Jesus asking me to extend the great love and reverence I have for Him to His body, the church, for which He shed His blood. It wasn't that I could think of any particular thing I was doing to damage His body, but until that day, I had no idea how seriously Christ takes the health and unity of His church.

Jesus reveals His passionate heart for unity in John 17:20–24:

> My prayer is . . . that all of them may be one, Father, just as you are in me and I am in you. May they be in us so that the world may believe that you sent me . . . May they be brought to complete unity to let the world know that you sent me and that you have loved them even as you have loved me.

Yes, I was already familiar with this passage, and it has been an important one to me that always motivated me to work towards unity in Christ's body. But when God spoke to me from 1 Corinthians 3:16–17, I saw deeper into His heart and purpose than I had before. I saw His love for His church, and I had a more intense appreciation for the essential role unity plays in reaching the world for Him. It caused me to *weep*! And it awakened in me a greater reverence and regard for His holiness. The disunity of the body of Christ is destructive to the health of churches, to individuals in the churches (see 1 Corinthians 11:20–30), and to the church's mission to reach the world for Christ. Worst of all, it breaks His heart.

In saying all this, I must reiterate the importance of biblical truth. We must never preserve unity at the expense of biblical truth. Those who dilute the truth of the gospel for unity's sake *miss the point of what unity is about*. Sometimes, sadly, unity cannot be achieved or preserved, in spite of our earnest efforts; things happen beyond our control, and though we try our best to maintain unity, we just can't seem to pull it off. God's Word encourages us, "*If* it is possible, *as far as it depends on you*, live at peace with everyone" (Romans 12:18). Nevertheless, we who do agree on who Jesus Christ is, what His gospel is, what our mission is; *we* who know him, revere his Word, and have experienced the life of his Holy Spirit; *we* are the ones who are far more accountable to God for living out these truths than are those who've never experienced them. May the Spirit of God *quicken us!* May He awaken us to the importance of love and unity in His Spirit. We must repent of pride-based teachings that build up *our* group and put others down.

We must also learn to refrain from judging other Christians, churches, and denominations for having different understandings and experiences of the Holy Spirit than our own. Carnal joking and caricatures about fellow Christians and churches are, in my opinion, no less offensive than the racial and gender slurs hurled at minorities and women. May we all together, and in one accord, humble ourselves and seek God for the fullness of His Spirit,[11] so that we as individuals, families, and churches (both local and worldwide) may be truly Spirit-filled, to the glory of God!

> Make every effort to keep the unity of the Spirit through the bond of peace. (Ephesians 4:3)
>
> And over all these virtues put on love, which binds them all together in perfect unity. (Colossians 3:14)

[11] See Chapter 7 "How To Be Filled With the Holy Spirit."

Chapter 5

What About Speaking in Tongues?

We come now to what one author has called "the biggest Christian friendship and oneness buster of the century"[12]—that is, speaking in tongues. I believe it is impossible to write seriously about the gift of the Holy Spirit and being filled with the Holy Spirit without including a significant discussion on the gift of speaking in tongues. One of my most prominent purposes for writing this book is to present a biblical approach to understanding the Holy Spirit that will bring evangelical Christians together as one body in Christ rather than contributing to their theological and functional division. We cannot accomplish this purpose unless we deal straightforwardly with the subject of speaking in tongues.

Perhaps my insights will not seem radically new or different, but hopefully my approach, growing out of an earnest desire to see Christ's body come together, will serve to form a solid common ground where we can see this desire realized. If the term "the baptism in the Holy Spirit" presents a challenge to unity for evangelical Christians, then "the gift of tongues" does so—*doubly!*

Reasons for Controversy

Reason #1—Tongues seem "strange"

"Tongues"—even the *name* sounds peculiar. And the very thought of speaking seemingly incoherent syllables out loud that even

---

[12] George Malone, *Those Controversial Gifts* (Downers Grove, IL: InterVarsity Press, 1983), 79.

the speaker doesn't understand sounds unusual, to say the least. It may seem even a little "weird," especially to our modern rational mindset. And yet, there it is in the Bible. Being Bible-believing Christians, we know we can't ignore it but must deal with it. Some of the controversy surrounding the gift of tongues, also called *glossalalia*, no doubt comes from the strangeness, the "unknown," the uncertainty about giving our vocal chords and tongues to something that the rational mind finds meaningless and perhaps embarrassing and even a little frightening.

I remember a time in my early Christian life when the thought of speaking in tongues seemed spooky to me. My concept of speaking in tongues was that the "Holy Ghost" (emphasizing the name for Him that caused me to fear the "unknown" about Him) suddenly comes upon a person and forces him to rattle off unintelligible gibberish. At times I would venture out into the unknown a little to pray, "Okay, Holy Spirit, you can give me the gift of tongues." Then, fearing that some irrational force would overtake me, I would invariably, and quickly, change my mind and say, "*NO! Don't do it!*" I know now that the Holy Spirit does not operate that way, but such was my fear at the time.

My misconceptions about speaking in tongues are probably fairly common among those who have not had much exposure to this gift. Not only did I see no need or purpose for it — the very thought of doing it frightened me. Besides, I knew the Holy Spirit was in my life. Furthermore, back then none of my Christian friends spoke in tongues. So I simply pushed it aside and forgot it for a while.

Reason #2—The Importance Attached to Tongues

My first real encounter with a tongues speaker who thought I should speak in tongues was as the Interim College Minister at a large Baptist church in Southern California. Our college group went in with First Baptist, Van Nuys and a number of other churches to provide an evangelistic outreach in Palm Springs during spring break. About three hundred of us stayed in the homes of local Christians for the week. I stayed with a Pentecostal woman and her Presbyterian husband. She conversed with me about speaking in tongues and asked me if I would like to discuss the subject with her pastor so I could learn more about it. I agreed to go with her. Both she and her pastor seemed to think it was *very important* that I speak in tongues. The pastor showed me a number of Scriptures, but nothing seemed to click in my mind as to *why* speaking in tongues was so significant. I remember asking, "What *good* does it do to speak in tongues?" Their answers didn't seem to make sense to me, and nothing they said made me want to speak in tongues. Yet, they still contended that it was very important that I receive this gift.

During that week in Palm Springs, I sadly observed a substantial amount of friction between her and her husband. It seemed to me that a lot of this friction was due to their different spiritual interests. He seemed like a nominal Christian without much spiritual understanding or motivation. She, on the other hand, was vastly more "spiritual" in her interests. She was so spiritual that she refused to concern herself with such mundane tasks as washing dishes and dirty clothes. No doubt this wife's air of spiritual superiority made her husband feel spiritually inferior. I left Palm Springs feeling that if tongues were truly from God, this woman would have seen better results in both her life and marriage. I reckoned that a valid spiritual gift would serve to build up and not divide a family.

This woman and her pastor typify *many* Christians who believe that speaking in tongues is very important—even *necessary* for Spirit-filled living; yet few of them can articulately explain the nature or purpose or benefits of speaking in tongues. Questions over the importance of speaking in tongues have divided the evangelical community. Thus, we have long suffered from an unresolved controversy.

When you have some Christians saying, "Tongues is *the* initial evidence for the baptism in the Holy Spirit," and others saying, "Tongues isn't for today," you're going to have controversy. Of course, these aren't even the most extreme positions—these are the mainstream ones. But look at this one: "You must speak in tongues to be saved, since the Bible says you aren't saved unless you have the Holy Spirit, and you don't have the Holy Spirit unless you can speak in tongues." And contrast that with this: "Tongues are not of God, they are of Satan since the Spirit doesn't do such things today." Pretty extreme, huh? Yet some people actually espouse these positions.

Most evangelical Christians probably fit into one or the other of two general positions: First, there are those who believe that speaking in tongues is a *necessary* experience for being filled with the Spirit. Second, there are others who believe that tongues is a valid spiritual gift, but that it is "the least important" of all the gifts, certainly not necessary, and for the most part not even desirable.

Reason #3: Different Practices of Tongues

Our theology will generally be expressed in our behavior; at least that is the idea—that we will live out what we profess. When we come to the practice of tongues, our theological differences move us to pursue vastly different experiences and practices. This results in serious controversy and division in Christ's body. Some churches, organizations, and denominations *forbid* speaking in tongues entirely. They forbid anyone who speaks in tongues, even in his or her personal prayer life, to exercise leadership in their churches or organizations. Other churches, organizations, and denominations are just the opposite: A person who does not believe that tongues is *the* initial evidence of being baptized in the Holy Spirit and who does not actually speak in tongues cannot serve in a leadership capacity.

Convictions and emotions surrounding the gift of tongues often run deep. The body of Christ needs a major move of God to heal the wounds and overcome the barriers to true unity regarding these issues. We need to admit the seriousness of our problem and realize that although *we* may be content with our present band-aid solutions in our own camps, *God* is not. We are like a married couple who, because they cannot get along, elect to have their own individual bedrooms. This seems like a workable solution to them, but to anyone who tours their home and observes their lifestyle, they are perceived as having serious marital problems that call for intense counseling and prayer.

I can't help but come back to what I said in the Introduction: If the Holy Spirit was given, in large measure, to build up and unite the body of Christ, then His working in and among us can be taught in a way that accomplishes this purpose. If this is true with the Holy Spirit's ministry in general, it is also true with the gift of speaking in tongues. The controversy and division over this gift is not attributable to the gift itself; it comes instead from our own faulty perceptions, unbalanced practices, and—*particularly* when we are dealing with tongues—*a whole lot of pride.*

More than we have yet realized or been willing to admit—it is this culprit, pride, that has pushed us into such rigidly fixed divisions. What explanation other than *pride* can explain our proneness to absolutize our own experience to the point that we say, "*Everyone* should speak in tongues," on the one hand, or, *"No one* should speak in tongues," on the other? Efforts to biblically substantiate *either* position are very weak, as we will see; but the tendency of the sinful human nature toward self-aggrandizement is *anything but weak!*

Many questions arise from these controversies surrounding the gift of tongues. Some of these we will seek to answer; although it would take an entire book to do justice to answering them all. In the following pages I will try to answer these questions: Is the gift of tongues for today? If "yes ," is it available to all believers? What does it mean to speak in tongues? Is speaking in tongues beneficial or purposeful? Is "tongues" really "the least of the gifts"? If so, what does that mean?

Is the Gift of Tongues for Today?

Most evangelical scholars and leaders acknowledge that the gift of tongues is a valid gift of the Holy Spirit today. Billy Graham—as mainstream an evangelical as anyone can be—wrote, "I personally cannot find any biblical justification for saying the gift of tongues was meant exclusively for New Testament times."[13] The late evangelical scholar (and one of my seminary professors), Dr. Bernard Ramm, wrote, "According to 1 Corinthians 12–14, and according to the witness of contemporary charismatics . . . this speaking in tongues is for worship, edification, and personal devotions. This is apparently the legitimate and proper use of tongues in the Christian fellowship."[14]

Significant numbers of evangelical Christians, however, are "cessationists," or dispensationalists. They believe that tongues and other miraculous gifts ceased after the apostolic period or in conjunction with the coming together of New Testament writings into the official New Testament canon. Cessationist George Zeller, tells us that Paul's teaching to not forbid tongues "no longer applies today."[15] All evangelical Christians agree that spiritual gifts are temporary in that we will not need spiritual gifts in heaven. Yet, while the great majority of Bible scholars believe that the sign gifts are for use in the church until Christ returns, the cessationists believe they have long since died out, no more to be seen. The primary Scripture cessationists like to use for substantiating their belief is:

> Love never fails. But where there are prophecies, they will cease; where there are tongues, they will be stilled; where there is knowledge, it will pass away. For we know in part and we prophesy in part, but when perfection comes, the imperfect disappears. When I was a child, I talked like a child, I thought like a child, I reasoned like a child. When I became a man, I put childish ways behind me. Now we see but a poor reflection as in a mirror; then we shall see face to face.
> (1 Corinthians 13:8-12)

---

[13] Graham, 172.

[14] Bernard L. Ramm, *Rapping About the Spirit* (Waco, TX: Word Books, 1974), 115.

[15] George W. Zeller, *God's Gift of Tongues: The Nature, Purpose and Duration of Tongues as Taught in the Bible* (Eugene, OR: Wipf and Stock Publishers, 2005), 104.

The cessationists interpret "*the perfect thing*" to be one of two things: One, the finished New Testament, or two, the matured Christian church. But the context of the passage clearly points to perfection, *full* and *complete* maturity, knowledge, etc. Believing that Paul meant anything short of the full realization of the Kingdom of God following the Second Coming of Jesus Christ seems impossible. The reading of the passage so naturally points to this that it would seem a person must already be committed to the cessationist position in order to come to that conclusion.

Gordon Fee and Douglas Stuart say this about the biased interpretation of this passage:

> . . . the most frequent justification for disregarding the imperatives about seeking spiritual gifts in 1 Corinthians 14 is a particular interpretation of 1 Corinthians 13:10, which states that, "when the perfect comes, the imperfect will pass away" (RSV). We are told that the perfect *has* come, in the form of the New Testament, and therefore the imperfect (prophecy and tongues) have ceased to function in the church. *But this is one thing the text cannot mean* because good exegesis totally disallows it. There is no possible way Paul could have meant that—after all, his readers did not know there was going to be a New Testament, and the Holy Spirit would not have allowed Paul to write something totally incomprehensible to them.[16]

Robert Graves lists a very impressive number (71!) of commentaries on 1 Corinthians—enough to consider it a *consensus* of reputable *non-Pentecostal commentators*—that view "the perfect thing" in verse 10 as "yet to come."[17] Those who look in the Bible for passages to support the view that the gift of tongues is not for today must resort

---

[16] Gordon D. Fee and Douglas Stuart, *How to Read the Bible for All Its Worth* (Grand Rapids, MI: Zondervan Publishing Co., 2003), 74.

[17] Robert W. Graves, *Praying in the Spirit* (Ada, MI: Chosen Books, 1987), 108-109.

to biblically unsubstantiated biases and speculations. Whereas, the Scriptures say *explicitly*, "Do not forbid speaking in tongues" (1 Corinthians 14:39).

Is the Gift of Speaking in Tongues for All Believers?

Most Pentecostals and charismatics say "yes." Citing the several Acts passages where speaking in tongues accompanied receiving the gift of the Holy Spirit, mainstream Pentecostal/charismatic theology teaches tongues as a normative experience, intended for all believers. *The Full Life Study Bible (An Interdenominational Study Bible for Pentecostal and Charismatic Christians)* states in its teaching notes on "Baptism in the Holy Spirit" (Acts 1:5):

> In the book of Acts, *speaking in tongues* . . . is the initial outward sign accompanying the baptism in the Holy Spirit (Acts 2:4–10, 45–46; 19:6). Baptism in the Holy Spirit is linked so closely with the external manifestation of *speaking in tongues* that this *should be considered the norm* when receiving the baptism.[18]

Robert Graves, in his book, *Praying in the Spirit,* writes "The Baptism in the Holy Spirit, which is evidenced by tongues-speaking, is *for all believers.*" But does the Bible substantiate this? The apostle Paul asks rhetorically, "Do all speak in tongues?" (1 Corinthians 12:30). For most evangelicals, the context makes it clear his answer is "No." However, the Pentecostals reply that Paul was referring to the public gift of tongues as messages brought forth in worship services rather than private prayer in tongues. It is true that 1 Corinthians 14 does describe two uses for the gift of tongues — public and private. However, it is *speculation* to interpret Paul's question, "Do all speak in tongues?" as dealing with the public gift only.

---

[18] Donald C Stamps, *NIV Full Life Study Bible* (Grand Rapids, MI: Zondervan Publishing Co., 1992), 1642.

Not a single New Testament Scripture teaches that all believers should receive the gift of tongues or that they can if they want to. Several groups spoke in tongues after they received the gift of the Spirit; for example, the 120 in the Upper Room on Pentecost (see Acts 2); the Gentiles in the home of Cornelius (see Acts 10); and the Ephesian "disciples" (see Acts 19); but these accounts do not constitute grounds for teaching that all Christians must, should, or can speak in tongues. Larry Hurtado writes:

> The most that anyone could legitimately infer—is that these phenomena were all familiar features of early Christian spiritual life and were manifestations of the Holy Spirit . . . One might suggest also that such phenomena are therefore regarded as among the legitimate "biblical" manifestations of the Spirit in the continuing progress of the gospel and life of the churches. *But the claim that these passages reflect a fixed doctrine* of how the Spirit is to be received in the lives of believers, including a doctrine of "initial evidence" of the Spirit's reception, *has no basis in the apparent intention of the author of Acts.*[19]

We find no evidence that tongues should be forbidden, but neither do we find evidence that tongues is normative for all believers. While the book of Acts describes the reception of tongues, it does not provide us with much teaching about tongues. Most of the *teaching* we have about tongues in the New Testament is in 1 Corinthians 12–14, where Paul corrects the Corinthian church for their *misuse* of the gift. (We should be thankful for their errors, without which we would know very little about the ongoing use of tongues in the lives of individual believers or in the church.)

---

[19] Larry Hurtado, "Normal but Not a Norm," *Initial Evidence: Historical and Biblical Perspectives on the Pentecostal Doctrine of Spirit Baptism*, ed. Gary B. McGee, (Peabody, MA: Hendrickson Publishers, 1991), 195.

Paul includes tongues in his list of valid spiritual gifts (1 Corinthians 12:10). Further, he wrote, "I would like all of you to speak in tongues" (14:5). He also made it clear that he spoke in tongues in his personal prayer life and valued the gift very highly: "I thank God that I speak in tongues more than all of you" (14:18). Even though he favored the gift of prophecy above tongues in public worship, he wrote emphatically, "Do *not forbid* speaking in tongues" (14:39). Nevertheless, he never said that all believers *could* speak in tongues or *should* speak in tongues. Neither did he teach anything that would substantiate the view that tongues was the initial evidence of receiving the Spirit. Nor did he link speaking in tongues as in any way essential to spiritual maturity or necessary for living a Spirit-filled life. On the contrary, he made it clear that speaking in tongues is of *no* value unless a person has love (1 Corinthians 13:1).

I personally speak in tongues (see "My Personal Experience with Tongues" in Chapter 6), and I greatly appreciate this gift. But I cannot go beyond the Scriptures. I cannot make my experience normative for all believers; only the Scriptures can do that, but they do not! I can say with Paul, "I *wish* that you all spoke in tongues" and "I thank God that I speak in tongues." I cannot, however, be honest with the Scriptures and at the same time conclude, "Every Christian ought to speak in tongues."

Tongues is a valuable spiritual gift although often misunderstood and misused. Nowhere does Scripture present it as a "litmus test" for being Spirit-filled or spiritually mature. Who can have this gift? Those to whom the Holy Spirit chooses to give it (1 Corinthians 12:7–11). I do not see in Scripture or in Christian experience where everyone can receive this gift. I have read that even in Pentecostal churches, where tongues is considered *essential* and *normative*, an average of 40 to 50 percent of those attending do not have this gift. I believe that many people have been damaged by the insistence that they can or should speak in tongues, when in fact they have tried and desperately want to but have not. To assert that these many sisters and brothers simply don't have enough faith, or are not humble enough, or are inhibited by fear or something else seems insensitive and unfair.

Even so, I am convinced that far more believers can have this gift than have received it. Millions of Christians don't even know that this gift is valid for today. The "Supernatural Gifts" package has been hidden from view (or they have been steered away from it!) in the bottom of the Holy Spirit Gift Box. Certainly nothing is wrong with learning about tongues and asking the Holy Spirit to give you that gift, or any other gift for that matter. Paul taught us to put love first, but also to "*eagerly desire spiritual gifts*" (1 Corinthians 14:1).

Peter Wagner has contributed a great deal toward helping the evangelical church at large to understand the purpose and use of spiritual gifts. Nevertheless, I disagree with his following assertion:

> It must be remembered that the body of Christ is universal, with many local manifestations. Spiritual gifts are given to the body universal and therefore certain ones may or may not be found in every particular local part of the body. *This explains why, for example, a local church, or even an entire denomination may not have been given the gift of tongues, while other parts of the body might have it.*[20]

I believe that the lack of this gift in some local churches or denominations has much more to do with the lack of information about the gift, or lack of desire for it, than with the Holy Spirit's unwillingness to give it. As George Malone writes, "The gift of tongues—or any other gift—is not likely to come to anyone who believes these gifts have ceased."[21] Jesus said, "According to your faith, it will be done to you" (Matthew 9:29).

We have concluded that the gift of tongues is available to the church today just as it was in the early church and that it is a normal

[20] Peter Wagner, *Frontiers in Mission Strategy* (Chicago: Moody Press, 1971), 71.
[21] Malone, 97.

but not normative experience. We now turn our attention to what speaking in tongues means.

What Does It Mean to Speak in Tongues?

Near universally recognized differences exist between the speaking in tongues we see in Acts 2 on the Day of Pentecost and the speaking in tongues Paul discusses in 1 Corinthians 12–14. The primary differences are these:

First, in Acts 2, the tongues were *known* languages that the "pre-Christian" hearers understood:

> When they heard this sound, a crowd came together in bewilderment, because each one heard them speaking in his own language. Utterly amazed, they asked: "Are not all these men who are speaking Galileans? Then how is it that each of us hears them in his own native language? . . . we hear them declaring the wonders of God in our own tongues!" (Acts 2:6–11)

In 1 Corinthians 14, on the other hand, the tongues that Paul described were *not* languages known to people but, rather, mysteries spoken to God. "For anyone who speaks in a tongue does not speak to men but to God. Indeed, no one understands him; he utters mysteries with his spirit" (1 Corinthians 14:2).

Second, the Acts 2 speaking in tongues accompanied *the initial outpouring of the Spirit* on the Day of Pentecost. In 1 Corinthians 12–14, Paul discusses tongues, not as a sign of the Holy Spirit's initial activity or presence in the lives of believers but as an *ongoing spiritual gift*. This ongoing spiritual gift of tongues manifests itself in two different ways. First, we find the *public* gift of tongues, which came as an inspired utterance in the context of a public worship service, accompanied by the gift of interpretation (14:9, 13; 14:27–28). Second, we see tongues as a personal gift, often called today a "prayer language," for use in one's personal prayer life: "For anyone who speaks in a tongue . . . (speaks) . . . to God . . . For if I *pray* in a tongue, my spirit prays..." (14:2, 14). Paul infers that nearly all of his own speaking in tongues was in his personal prayer life: "I thank God that I speak in tongues more than all of you. *But in the church* I would rather speak five intelligible words to instruct others than ten thousand words in a tongue" (14:18–19).

What is the nature of this praying in tongues? Paul says: "For if I pray in a tongue, *my spirit* prays, but my mind is unfruitful. So what shall I do? *I will pray with my spirit*, but I will also pray with my mind; *I will sing with my spirit*, but I will also sing with my mind" (14:14–15). This passage tells us that when a person prays in tongues, his *human spirit* is praying, rather than his mind. The Scriptures teach that human beings have three interrelated dimensions: the body, the soul, and the spirit. Paul points these out in 1 Thessalonians 5:23 when he prays a blessing on the Christians of Thessalonica: "May God Himself, the God of peace, sanctify you through and through. May your whole *spirit* and *soul* and *body* be kept sound and blameless at the coming of our Lord Jesus Christ." The author of Hebrews also points to a distinction between soul and spirit when he writes: "For the word of God is living and active. Sharper than any double-edged sword, it penetrates even to dividing *soul* and *spirit*" (4:12).

Since Scripture does not precisely define spirit, soul, and body, we can only "paint with broad strokes" as we try to understand their meaning. The *body* is the easiest to comprehend: our physical bodies. The *spirit* is the deepest part of us, that part which has the capacity to know God. The spirit is considered to be dead or dormant prior to our coming to know Christ. Paul writes:

> As for you, *you were dead* in your transgressions and sins in which you used to live when you followed the ways of this world and of the ruler of the kingdom of the air . . . But because of his great love for us, God, who is rich in mercy, *made us alive* with Christ *even when we were dead* in transgressions. (Ephesians 2:1, 2, 5).

Before we become Christians, we are *spiritually* dead. Our bodies are alive, as are our minds and emotions, but our *spirits* are dead to God. We do have the capacity to be spiritually alive; after all, we were made in God's image, chosen and predestined by God "to be adopted as his sons through Jesus Christ (Ephesians 1:4–5). But *sin* has resulted in spiritual death (Romans 6:23). When a person responds in faith to Jesus Christ, a miracle of the Spirit takes place by which that person, previously dead in spirit, is born spiritually. He or she becomes spiritually alive. The Gospel of John describes this experience in John 3:3–6:

> In reply Jesus declared, "I tell you the truth, no one can see the Kingdom of God unless he is born again . . . No one can enter the kingdom of God unless he is born of water and the Spirit. Flesh gives birth to flesh, but *the Spirit gives birth to spirit.*"

Flesh giving birth to flesh obviously describes the physical birth that all human beings experience. Their parents conceive them, and they are born physically. The *spiritual* birth, "Spirit gives birth to spirit," takes place when a person receives Christ as Savior and Lord. Previously dead, the spirit is now made alive and indwelt by the Spirit of God.

Summarizing, we understand the *body* is our physical being and the *spirit* is the deepest part of us, once dead but now alive in Christ. The *soul,* then, is everything else — namely, our minds, emotions, wills, and so forth. When I pray in tongues, I am not praying with my mind; that is, I am not forming and articulating words and concepts that I understand; rather, I am praying with my spirit. When I pray in tongues, the deepest part of my being, my human spirit, now alive in Christ, *communicates directly to God, spirit to Spirit.*

Praying in tongues is not an uncontrollable, ecstatic utterance, during which the person praying is "beside himself" or in some kind of trance. The person praying is able to pray or not pray, to start and stop at will; otherwise, Paul's instructions concerning the use of tongues would make no sense. Concerning the public gift of tongues, Paul writes: "If there is no interpreter, the speaker should keep quiet" (1 Corinthians 14:28). Obviously, the speaker could choose to speak or not speak. The same is true with a personal prayer language. At times, the indwelling Holy Spirit inspires such prayer, both in public and in private. However, the Holy Spirit is gentle, not coercive; He inspires, and motivates, but He does not coerce or possess, as happens with demonic possession.

Is Speaking in Tongues Beneficial or Purposeful?

Paul tells us in 1 Corinthians 14 that praying in tongues is both beneficial and purposeful. First, praying in tongues edifies the speaker: "He who speaks in a tongue *edifies himself*" (14:4). Being spiritually edified is a very good thing. In fact, all spiritual gifts have this in common: the Spirit gives them to edify believers. Tongues is unique among the spiritual gifts in that it focuses upward in worship to God, rather than outward toward other believers. It is unique also in that its primary use is personal and private rather than corporate and public. When we exercise the gift of tongues in personal prayer, we obviously focus our prayer toward God, just as when we are praying in our native or learned language. And, just as when we pray in our native language, spending time with God in tongues-prayer personally builds us up spiritually. There is nothing at all wrong with that! Building ourselves up spiritually is vitally important. When we spend time alone with God in His Word, for example, we seek in large part to build ourselves up spiritually.

Every evangelical Christian leader and church knows how important it is to spend time with God in prayer and in His Word; but *many* evangelicals have missed this point when it comes to praying in tongues. Comments like this one by Billy Graham, are very common among evangelicals:

> . . . the gift of tongues mentioned in 1 Corinthians 12–14 is clearly one of the less important gifts of the Spirit—in fact it appears to be the least important. The reason for this is that it often does not give any spiritual benefit to other believers. The other gifts clearly are exercised to build up and strengthen the body of Christ.[22]

Billy Graham certainly has been a wonderful, gifted, anointed man of God whom I esteem more highly than words can express. However, it seems to me that statements like this show the need for a paradigm shift among evangelical teachers and leaders. The Scriptures do not tell us that tongues is "the least of the gifts." When evaluating the *public* use of tongues, it is clear that Paul prefers those gifts, like prophecy, which are intelligible and therefore beneficial to other believers. But concerning the *private* use of tongues in one's personal devotional life, he offers no "rating," and he certainly doesn't call it "the least" of the gifts.

Sometimes I hear evangelical leaders say, "Well, after all, tongues is "the least of the gifts." When I hear this, I feel they are implying, "Since it's the *least* of the gifts it's not worth having." How sad! In the first place, *it's presumptuous to think that the Holy Spirit would bother to give God's children ANY gift not worth having.* Besides, if this gift is "least" or unimportant, why would Paul spend so much time praying in tongues, and why was he so thankful for the gift (1 Corinthians 14:18)? As I have mentioned, this attitude ignores the distinction between *personal* prayer in tongues and the *public* gift of tongues.

Can you imagine an evangelical leader asserting that the *personal* use of God's Word in private devotions is "the least important" use of God's Word and that the better use of His Word is in public preaching and Bible studies? I can't either. Obviously, building oneself up spiritually in personal Bible study and devotion serves a vital role, and so does the corporate use of God's Word to build up Christ's

---

[22] Graham, 173.

body. Just because something is used *primarily* for *personal* spiritual edification rather than for the edification of Christ's body, does not mean it is unimportant or undesirable. It simply has a distinct purpose. Besides, *personal* edification, whether through Bible devotions or through praying in tongues, has the indirect effect of building up the church. It goes without saying that spiritually edified believers edify the church far more than those who are *not* personally edified.

We have seen that praying in tongues is beneficial because it edifies the one praying. But is it *purposeful*? What kind of praying is it? *How* does it edify? When we pray in tongues, it is true that we do not know *what* we are praying. We must assume, however, that *any* form of Spirit-inspired prayer is purposeful, whether we understand the purpose or not. And certainly *God* knows what we are praying. C.H. Dodd asserts: "An inarticulate aspiration is itself the work of the divine in us, and though we ourselves may not be conscious of its meaning, God knows what it means, and answers the prayer."[23] Paul explains in Romans 8:26-27:

> In the same way, the Spirit helps us in our weakness. We do not know what we ought to pray for, but the Spirit himself intercedes for us with groans that words cannot express. And he who searches our hearts knows the mind of the Spirit, because the Spirit intercedes for the saints in accordance with God's will.

I don't believe that Paul is here identifying the Spirit's intercession for us as speaking in tongues exclusively. Nevertheless, we have every reason to believe that this is *at least one of the means* the Holy Spirit can use to do it. Often we have burdens and unresolved conflicts deep within us, sometimes deeper than our mind's ability to understand or articulate in prayer. Praying in tongues bypasses the mind

---

[23] C.H. Dodd, *The Epistle of Paul to the Romans* (London: Hadder Stoughton, 1932), 135; quoted by Malone, 85.

and provides us the opportunity to communicate from our deepest being directly to God. Through our praying in tongues, the Holy Spirit is free to focus His intercession in whatever direction He chooses—He can pray for us and our personal needs, and He can also pray for the needs of others. Paul's exhortation in Ephesians 6:18 to "pray in the Spirit at all times" is within the context of spiritual warfare. Though prayer "in the Spirit" encompasses both prayer in tongues and prayer in one's native language, this passage is sufficient to suggest that praying in tongues is a useful weapon of intercession and catalyst for victory when we are engaged in spiritual warfare.

In addition to the Spirit's ministry of interceding through us, we know also that praying in tongues is a form of *praise* and *thanksgiving*: Paul writes:

> If you are praising God with your spirit, how can one who finds himself among those who do not understand say "Amen" to your thanksgiving, since he does not know what you are saying? You may be giving thanks well enough, but the other man is not edified. (1 Corinthians 14:16–17)

The gift of tongues is primarily a *worship* gift, uniquely *God-ward* in focus, and characterized by *praise and thanksgiving* to God. Although the tongues in Acts 2 and the tongues in 1 Corinthians 14 differ in most respects, they have this in common: in essence, the purpose of both is to offer *praise* to God. This is obviously true of the 1 Corinthians 14 gift in the passage above, and in Acts 2:11 where we observe the same purpose on the Day of Pentecost when the pre-Christians declared in amazement, "We hear them *declaring the wonders of God* in our own tongues."

A New Paradigm Shift Needed

Again, we need a paradigm shift within Christ's body. In the context of understanding tongues as a uniquely God-focused gift of praise and worship, what does it mean to say that tongues is "the least of the gifts"?

The Holy Spirit continually moves within God's people, both individually and corporately, in three directions. He moves in the *outward* direction in evangelistic mission and service in the world. He also moves in the *inward* direction, to build Christ's body through creating Christ-centered fellowship and distributing spiritual gifts for use in building up the church. And He moves in the *upward* direction, inspiring worship and praise to God. I believe it is obvious, both in the Scriptures and in our Christian experience, that the Holy Spirit moves in these three directions, continuously, simultaneously, and interrelatedly.

We see in Scripture that the Holy Spirit inspires mission. He empowers for witness (Acts 1:8), initiates evangelistic mission (Acts 13:1–2), and calls and equips some to the ministry of evangelism (Ephesians 4:11). In addition, He works miracles in conjunction with the preaching of the gospel. We also see clearly His role in building the body of Christ (inward focus). At Pentecost He created a Christian community of 3,000 believers who were "together" daily, committed to fellowship, and who shared everything they had with one another (Acts 2:42–47). They were "one in heart and mind" (Acts 4:32). He also distributes gifts for building up the body of Christ (1 Corinthians 12:4–31; Romans 12:4–8; 1 Peter 4:10).

The entire evangelical church generally recognizes the Holy Spirit's role in these first two directions—outward (mission) and inward (fellowship and body life). Yet, when it comes to the Holy Spirit's *upward* direction, that of worship and praise to God, we have been slow to catch on. The Scriptures clearly reveal that the Holy Spirit is the "Prime Mover" here, too. He inspired the writing of the Psalms, a book of praise and worship songs. (We can see the present-day move of God's Spirit that has resulted in thousands of new songs of praise and worship that are circling the globe). The Spirit inspired David to make 400 musical instruments for use in worship (see 2 Chronicles 29:25–30). And in the New Testament, Paul points to the

Holy Spirit's role of inspiring Spirit-filled worship: "Be filled with the Spirit. Speak to one another with psalms, hymns and spiritual songs. Sing and make music in your heart to the Lord" (Ephesians 5:18-20).

Our behavior, however, both in our personal lives as well as in corporate worship, often betrays us. How many of us are really *worshipers?* Are we more concerned about our choice of songs; the musical arrangements; the professionalism of the worship team; our various tools, techniques, and technologies than we are of true heartfelt worship of God? How many of our churches have the mechanics down to the point where we can actually pull off an impressive worship service without the Holy Spirit participating at all? Worship is not about us—our abilities, our enjoyment, our preferences. It's about God. It's about loving Him, honoring Him, welcoming His presence, and blessing His heart.

Worship, of course, begins with committing ourselves to God (Romans 12:1) and with acknowledging and serving Him in every area of our lives. But shouldn't a heart that claims to be filled with the Spirit of worship, desire to spend quality time in pure God-focused praise and adoration? Shouldn't our fervent emotions as well as our rational minds be involved in expressing our love and adoration directly to God? Aren't such expressions of praise to God *important*? Of course they are!

Seen in the context of the Holy Spirit's role in worship, the gift of speaking in tongues takes on entirely new significance. Tongues is, first and foremost, a gift of the Spirit that releases heartfelt and Spirit-led praise and worship. I have a theory that grows out of these Biblical truths: The gift of tongues not only releases individual Christians who use it privately into new dimensions of praise and worship; the gift also has a powerful catalyst effect on the corporate body's praise and worship as these spiritually renewed individuals come together—*even when* the gift is not publicly exercised.

Surely, it must be obvious to all that great dissimilarities in depth and fervency of worship exist among churches. For example, one church may corporately sing "How Great Thou Art" or the chorus, "Shout to the Lord." The Lord's presence is very powerful, and a genuine spirit of worship permeates the sanctuary. Another church may sing the same songs, and, although they may sing beautifully, they seem to lack the fervency of heart and intensity of the Lord's presence. What makes the difference? I admit that the following point is speculative, but even so, based on my own experience and observation, I have come to believe the following: *Churches or Christian gatherings that view the gift of tongues as a valuable and welcome gift, and where a significant number of people present have received that gift, tend to experience worship times that are deeper and more powerful in God's felt presence than churches or Christian gatherings that view the gift of tongues as unimportant and where few if any have received that gift.* Again, I know that this is speculative, but if this observation becomes more generally acknowledged, I won't be surprised, because, as I have shown, the gift of speaking in tongues is *first and foremost a worship gift*.

In that the Holy Spirit moves in three directions—upward, inward, and outward to the glory of God—we should expect that various spiritual gifts operate in those three directions as well. This is born out in Scripture and also in our church experience. God gives numerous spiritual gifts for building the body and reaching the lost for Christ. He also gives some that are used in *worship*, such as singing, music, prophecy, tongues and interpretation, teaching, revelation (1 Corinthians 14:26ff). Of these, tongues is the only one that is totally God-focused and personal. The *interpretation* of tongues focuses on the body, but tongues itself is uniquely God-focused.

Now what significance does this have as we look at the context of Paul's teaching on tongues in 1 Corinthians 12–14? As we seek to understand the historical and literary context of these chapters, we see Paul's primary concern here is dealing with a church that prides itself in using spiritual gifts but that has completely lost sight of the Holy Spirit's *inward* ministry—that of building up Christ's body. They have caused serious divisions in the church by their false view of what it means to be Spirit-filled. Paul brings a word of correction to them. They need to *love* one another, to recognize the absolutely essential role of the Spirit in creating and maintaining the unity and health and upbuilding of the church. The *last* thing they need to concern themselves with is tongues.

But what if the context of our evangelical churches is different from the first-century Corinthian church? What if a church is fine in its understanding of body life and the importance of love and unity, but the church has a recognizably "dead" worship experience? Do you think Paul would tell them to keep studying the inward and outward roles of the Spirit but to ignore the upward role? Do you think He would tell them that tongues, the only uniquely God-focused worship gift is unimportant, or the least of the gifts? I think not. I recently had a conversation about this very point with Pastor Ed Owens of Olivet Baptist Church in East Lansing, Michigan. He affirmed the role of the gift of tongues as it relates to fostering the presence of God in worship in his own church, and he said, "The Holy Spirit's presence is very important in our worship experience. I have preached in other churches, and when it comes to the presence of the Spirit, there is a world of difference between churches."

Let me clarify something at this point. I am not saying here that people who pray in tongues are better or deeper worshipers than those who do not. Not at all! What I am saying, and what I believe, is that the gift of tongues is, in some way that I can't explain, a *catalyst* that has the power to release a deeper experience of worship in an entire gathering of believers. As the body gathers in worship, I believe the Spirit uses the worship release experienced in the lives of those who speak in tongues in their personal prayer lives to *release the Spirit of worship in the gathering as a whole.* This could explain why the Holy Spirit does not give this gift to everybody—it is not necessary that everyone have it. If what I am saying is true, it gives those with the gift of personal tongues a significant ministry in the body; God can use them to ignite a deeper experience of worship for all.

I believe that, overall, evangelical churches would greatly benefit by putting the gift of tongues in a more positive light and by encouraging their members to learn about it and to seek God for it as a prayer/praise gift for their personal devotional lives. Pastors who do not speak in tongues do not need to feel threatened by those in their churches who do, any more than a member with the gift of service should be threatened by the pastor's gift of preaching. We each have our own gifts and abilities. As long as we use them for building up rather than for tearing down, we should wholeheartedly affirm one another's gifts. What we need is a balanced theology of the Holy Spirit, where all the spiritual gifts find their rightful place, both in doctrine and in practice.

Chapter 6

My Personal Experience with Tongues

I have already described my initial encounter with someone who spoke in tongues — the Pentecostal woman in Palm Springs. That encounter left me with a "bad taste in my mouth," with regards to speaking in tongues. But something else happened later that completely changed my outlook and experience.

Two months after the Palm Springs outreach, I left my position as Interim College Minister in a large Baptist church to take a three-month assignment as a street missionary in Berkeley, California. Four of us "summer missionaries" from different parts of the country shared responsibilities in the "Telegraph Avenue Project," sponsored by the American Baptist Home Missions Society (now called National Ministries). The project included a meal program where 200-500 street people ate one meal five days a week; a runaway center; and a coffeehouse, where we talked, played cards, and listened to music. My primary area of responsibility was with the coffeehouse.

My Berkeley experiences profoundly affected me. I got to know multitudes of people from many walks of life I had only read about. I spent many hours with people who were mentally ill, misfits, drug addicts, ex-cons, anti-American revolutionaries, runaway teenagers, young black men from the Oakland ghetto. My strolls on the U.C. Berkeley campus never ceased to inform and amaze me. These ventures exposed me to seemingly countless ideologies, isms, and religions. (I kept a journal of my experiences that summer that got published with the title, *Berkeley Journal: Jesus and the Street-People, A First-Hand Report.*[24]

The intense experiences of that summer awakened me to a deep need in my life: If I truly wanted to make a dent in a place like Berkeley, I needed far more of the Holy Spirit's power and gifts. Working in Berkeley taught me a lot about how to relate to many different kinds of people. I also learned how to articulate the Christian faith and to speak from a Christian perspective to significant issues of the day. Yet, when I left Berkeley at the end of that summer to come home and continue my seminary education, I left with an intense awareness of my need for more of God in my life.

Prior to Berkeley, the measure of the Holy Spirit's activity in my life seemed sufficient. I did fine ministering to a group of well-adjusted middle and upper middle class evangelical church young people. Immersed in the street culture of radical, crazy *Berzerkly*, however, I felt like I had barely enough of the Holy Spirit's power to scratch the surface of what God wanted to do. I became convinced that I needed more of the Holy Spirit's power and gifts working in and through me.

Within several months of returning to seminary, I met Cheri, the woman who is now my wife. She and her two sisters were "Jesus Freaks," part of the enormous wave of God's Spirit in Southern California and elsewhere known as "The Jesus Movement." She and her sisters traveled several nights a week from Pomona to Costa Mesa, California to attend exciting meetings at Calvary Chapel.

Cheri invited me to join her for an evening meeting, so I went as an observer, just to check it out. Hundreds of people, mostly young adults and youth, crammed into the church. Hardly a square inch of free space remained in the building. Most noticeable was their freedom and joy in worship. I'd never witnessed anything like this before. I had always enjoyed singing hymns and choruses at church and fel-

---

[24] Clay Ford, *Berkeley Journal: Jesus and the Street-People, A First-Hand Report* (New York: Harper & Row, 1972).

lowship gatherings, but this was vastly different. Here was a depth and richness of worship and a greater intensity of God's presence during worship than I had ever before experienced. (Such was the case in the infancy of this movement.)

I had to visit again! The next time I progressed from detached observer to hungry participant. Drinking in the warmth and freedom that the Spirit of God brought about, I wanted to be part of it.

Cheri gave me a book to read about being filled with the Spirit and speaking in tongues.[25] I knew I had received the Holy Spirit when I became a Christian, so I approached the book cautiously. The author asked the question, "Do you have to have this experience to be a Christian?" If his answer had been "Yes," I would have thrown the book away. But his answer was, "Certainly not." So I kept reading.

The book described "the baptism in the Holy Spirit" and tongues in the traditional Pentecostal way, and I didn't feel comfortable with that, even then. But I knew that I wanted and needed more of God's Spirit in my life. So I read on. As I recall, the author said something like, "Some people reject this filling with the Spirit and speaking in tongues because they see people misuse the gifts." He hit the nail on the head with that one. The spiritual pride I had seen in Palm Springs had turned me off. He continued, "Just like this, a lot of people reject Christ because they see hypocritical Christians." Hey! His point was clear and well taken: It is a mistake to reject an experience or gift from God *solely because* some people who have received it are unbalanced, immature, and divisive. In my previous negative experience with the teaching and attitudes of tongues-speakers, I had allowed my negative feelings to attach themselves to the gift of tongues as well. I had thrown out "the baby with the bath water."

When I finished reading the book, I went into my bedroom to pray. I didn't agree with everything the author had said, but he had addressed some of my primary questions and concerns. I wanted more

---

[25] Don Basham, *Handbook on Holy Spirit Baptism* (New Kensington, PA: Whitaker House, 1969).

of God in my life, and I was ready. So I started to pray. It was a conditional prayer that included a number of *if*s, something like this:

> Dear God, if this experience is of You, and if it will help me be more effective in ministering to other people, and if I am mature enough so that I won't look down my nose at others who don't have this gift, then I'd like to have this experience. I'd like to speak in tongues.

At that point, I stepped out in faith and began to speak in syllables I didn't understand. It seemed so natural and easy—*very* different from the frightening "take over" experience I had feared a year or two earlier. As I offered these syllables, I felt something happen. I felt the Holy Spirit's warm presence filling me, engulfing me. It was like God's Spirit and my spirit were moving in harmony together, more closely intertwined than I had ever experienced before. I tingled all over, and I felt like warm oil was moving up and down my spine. As I prayed in tongues, I felt an intense excitement in me. Even though I had no idea what I was saying, I knew that some very meaningful communion was taking place between me and my heavenly Father.

I share these "feeling" experiences, not because they are essential; *they are not* (some people don't "feel" much of anything when they pray in tongues yet find themselves spiritually edified). I share my experiences simply because they describe what happened to me personally when I prayed and stepped out in faith to receive this gift.

The next time I saw Cheri, I was bubbling over. I excitedly told her what happened after I read the book she gave me. Instead of sharing my joy, her countenance dropped into a sorrowful frown. Then, to my chagrin, she began to cry. "What's wrong?" I asked. "I thought you'd be excited!"

She poured out to me how she believed in the gift and had earnestly sought it but had not yet received it. She was very depressed about it, as if in some sense God had rejected her as unworthy of having this gift. Misguided, though well-meaning friends, no doubt, had caused many of these feelings. They pressured her and repeatedly laid hands on her in prayer, all to no avail. The prevalent view in her circle was that everyone *should* speak in tongues, and *could*—if they so desired. So when their prayers went unanswered, they had only one explanation to offer: Something was wrong with Cheri! Either she lacked faith, or demons hindered her, or she had emotional and psychological problems that prevented her from being released to exercise this gift. The woman she lived with even had a man with a gift of discernment come out to the house to pray and discern whether Cheri had the Holy Spirit in her life at all! This was extremely painful for Cheri who knew God had saved her but felt that He was somehow rejecting her in a key spiritual area of the Christian life. She wondered if He was offended with her or if she just plain was not good enough.

It is hard to see sincere Christians treated this way. There are people who *desperately* want to speak in tongues, some thinking their spiritual life depends on it. They seek it perpetually but still don't receive. Often they are made to feel like something is wrong with them; they're not "Spirit-filled," and therefore somehow inferior. I believe this kind of treatment of God's children needs to stop.

Several years later Cheri received a prayer language; but even had she not, her devotion to Christ, her zeal to witness, and her fervent intercession for revival made it clear that the Holy Spirit had already filled her.

Prayer Language: A Blessing in My Life

I have found my prayer language to be a tremendous blessing in my life. But before I share what some of those blessings are, I want to say this: God is able to bless His children who do *not* speak in tongues in similar ways, and He obviously does so. I see no need or reason for a "haves-versus-have-nots" perspective when it comes to the gift of speaking in tongues. Tongues do not make me or anyone else a better or more Spirit-filled Christian than one who does not possess this particular gift. Nevertheless, God has chosen to use this gift to bless and strengthen me and millions of others in a number of ways, all of which 1 Corinthians 14 describes.

First, praying in tongues edifies me spiritually. It is like a catalyst that gets my "spiritual juices" pumping, so to speak. One time I was driving alone on a three-hour trip to a pastor's conference. For some reason I was feeling despondent and far from God. So I began to pray in tongues, and after 15 minutes or so, my spirit felt somewhat rejuvenated. Then I started singing, moving back and forth between English and tongues. Well, you can guess what happened. God's Spirit flooded my heart, and it seemed that His presence filled my entire car. By the time I got to the conference I was *aglow* with the Spirit. I rejoiced as I continued to sing hymns and choruses and tongues of praise from a heart overflowing with love and gratitude to God. Over the years, I have had many similar experiences.

Praying in tongues has edified and stimulated my Christian life in other ways, too. Often I spend time praying in tongues as well as in English before I preach or minister to people. Praying in tongues seems to sharpen my spiritual sensitivity. It puts me in a place of spiritual readiness to be an instrument for other spiritual gifts. Frequently, after praying privately in tongues, I find myself praying for someone's very specific need when the person had never disclosed their need. Later, that person informed me that my prayer was "right on target."

I find that praying softly in tongues before a ministry session somehow makes me more available and ready for God to use me. The Holy Spirit has used me to give words of knowledge, wisdom, encouragement, and He has also used me in healing ministry.

Two particular experiences that link my prayer language to supernatural gifts of ministry come to mind. The first one concerned a wonderful man who was dying of leukemia. The members of his family were "pillars" in a church I pastored in Southern California. At age fifty-seven, without warning he was hospitalized with acute chronic leukemia. The grim prognosis devastated his family. Rarely have I seen an apparently healthy man go downhill so quickly. Within a short time he was in a coma with a respirator pumping oxygen into his lungs to keep him alive.

Of course, our entire church and numerous other friends and churches were praying. But his condition only continued to deteriorate. Doctors gave him a very short time to live. One was particularly negative in his prognosis: “I don’t believe he will live any more than 24 to 48 hours. Even if he does, his lungs have been destroyed by the nearly pure oxygen pumped into them to keep him alive.” The family, having learned of the illness just a few short weeks before, felt completely unprepared for his death.

I will never forget that Monday after Easter Sunday. It was my day off, but I felt the Holy Spirit prompting me to visit this man in the hospital. I felt a strong impression: “Today is the day. If he isn’t healed today, it’s over.” When I entered the room, his wife was standing over his bed praying. She looked at me and said, “Today is the day. If he isn’t healed today, it’s over.” “I know,” I replied.

I sat in a chair about ten feet from his bed and began praying softly in tongues. I did this for ten or fifteen minutes. At that point I felt impressed to go over to this dear man and to place my hand on his chest. As I did so, I spoke softly but with authority, “In the name of Jesus Christ, be healed.”

Often when praying for people, I feel nothing; I know from experience that feelings are not all that important. Sometimes miracles happen in answer to prayers that “feel” like they went nowhere. But this time—wow!—I literally *felt* the power of God go through my hand and into his chest. I saw no visible change—he still lay there in a coma. Yet I *knew* that something had happened, and I couldn’t wait to come back and see him the next day.

Sure enough, the following day he opened his eyes and gave me a big smile! He got better and better every day. The respirator prevented him from talking, so as he improved, he started communicating by pointing to letters. Soon, doctors removed the respirator. I recall with excitement that the doctors, after examining his lungs, reported that not only were his lungs not ruined, but they were as healthy as a teenager's! He went into remission. The family—and *all* of us who loved him deeply—got to keep him with us for another fifteen months. Another year of birthdays, Father's Day, Thanksgiving, Christmas. It was a delightful season. Then God, in His sovereign purpose, took him home. This time, the family had adequate time to say their goodbyes. They were grateful for the wonderful time they had all had together.

The second experience linking my prayer language with supernatural ministry took place in a convalescent home. I was the pastor at that time of a church located in a largely Hispanic area. One of the youngsters in the neighborhood had become a regular at our house there in the neighborhood. His grandmother was raising him; his mother had ridden off with the Hell's Angels when he was just a baby, and his father was in prison.

The grandmother, I'll call her "Marta," was a Catholic. We could see, even from the first time we met her, that she had frail health. The family problems, along with raising three lively grandsons, had worn her out before her time. Cheri and I had met this dear lady and had invited her to visit our church. Nevertheless, the occasion never arose for talking with her in-depth about spiritual things.

In time, we moved from that neighborhood, buying a house about five miles from the church. About two years later, I received a call from Marta's daughter, a Christian. She asked me to come and pray for her mom who was in a coma and not expected to live. She didn't think Marta had ever been born-again and was deeply concerned that she wouldn't go to heaven.

I arrived at the convalescent home and met her daughter and her pastor who had come from out of town. They had tried repeatedly to awaken Marta but without success. When I saw her, I grimaced at her extremely weak condition. She lay there comatose, her skin orange-colored. I also tried to wake her, but she remained unresponsive.

As the daughter and her pastor prayed across the room, I sat down beside Marta and prayed softly in tongues for about ten minutes. I felt impressed to speak her name, and I said forcefully but not loudly, "Marta." Immediately, her eyes opened. "Marta," I said, "This is Pastor Clay from the church." She seemed to recognize me. "Marta, I've come to pray for you. I'd like to lead you in a prayer. I know you are weak, so I don't expect you to pray this prayer out loud. Just say it in your heart, and trust Jesus to be your Savior." I then began to pray: "Lord Jesus . . ." To my amazement, she repeated, loudly and earnestly, "Lord Jesus." Excitedly, I led her, phrase by phrase, into a saving relationship with Jesus Christ. She acknowledged her need for Christ and thanked Him for dying on the cross to forgive her sins. She invited Him to come into her heart as Savior and Lord.

When I had finished the prayer, I said, "Amen." She repeated, "Amen." Then she closed her eyes and went back into her coma. I couldn't wake her after that, but even so the tears streaming down her cheeks shouted an unmistakable message: Marta was born again and going to heaven! She went home to be with Jesus that same week.

By God's sovereignty, the family chose me to do the funeral service, an open air service at the gravesite. There appeared to be two-hundred or more people present, including many gang members. One of her sons attended—I will never forget seeing him climb out of the sheriff's car with his feet in chains. I related to the crowd what had happened in Marta's life, how she had accepted Jesus. When I gave the same opportunity to those present, *scores* of people acknowledged Christ in prayer and invited Him to be their Savior.

Understandably, speaking in tongues has proved itself a precious gift to me. My prayer language helps prepare me spiritually for preaching, for evangelism, for ministry to people, and for spiritual warfare. When I sense that I am under spiritual attack, I will often spend a considerable amount of time, sometimes an hour or even two hours, praying in tongues. This does make a *significant* difference in my life. Again, I want to make it clear that what God does in my life through this means, He can do in the lives of those who don't speak in tongues by *other* means. Also, I must say I realize that praying in tongues is not a substitute for praying in English or for spending time in God's Word. I can "pray in the Spirit" (Ephesians 6:18), whether in

English or in tongues. And I would never even consider compromising or forsaking "the sword of the Spirit, which is the Word of God" (Ephesians 6:17).

The final major area of great blessing to me pertains to praise and worship. From the start of my Christian life, I've enjoyed singing praises to God. But receiving the gift of tongues worked to release in me a greater freedom and even greater joy in praising and worshiping God than I ever imagined.

The Holy Spirit is the quintessential Worshiper. He absolutely delights in adoring, honoring and glorifying the Father and the Son. As I have mentioned, tongues is, first and foremost, a *worship* gift. Praying in tongues somehow releases the Spirit of praise in me so that I am free to express my love to the Father and to my Lord Jesus at depths I had never plumbed before receiving this gift. And I have already expressed my observation and conviction that this gift, where appreciated, can act as a catalyst, releasing a rich Spirit of worship within an entire congregation.

I want to close this chapter by saying that I don't think that speaking in tongues makes me a better Christian than others who don't possess this gift. Nevertheless, I *do* know that it helps me and blesses me in many ways. I can join Paul in attesting, "I thank God I speak in tongues."

I would never try to force this gift upon someone or imply that they aren't where they should be if they don't have it. I don't subscribe to the belief that tongues is the initial evidence of receiving the gift of the Holy Spirit. I believe A *CHANGED LIFE* is that evidence! The Bible does not teach that every believer must, should, or could speak in tongues.

At the same time, however, it truly *grieves* me—and I'm sure it saddens the Holy Spirit, too—when my fellow believers ridicule, mock, and treat as repugnant this gift and those who use it. To insinuate that tongues is not of God so it must be fake or demonic in origin; or that it is foolish gibberish; or that only the poorly educated or hyper-emotional people get it or use it; or that it is invalid because it is not a language that conforms to the definitions of modern linguistic science; or even the old evangelical standby, "It's just the *least* of the gifts"—all these comments by my brothers and sisters in Christ are grievous. They belittle a precious gift that the Holy Spirit has given to me and to multiplied millions of Christians throughout the world.

Brothers and sisters in Christ, can't we place on God's altar our harsh, rigidly fixed, and often divisive approaches to understanding this gift? Often we arrive at our perspectives more by making absolutes of our own experiences than by accepting the balanced truth of God's Word.

Let me ask you personally, brother or sister in Christ, do you hold a position on this gift that contributes to the raising of barriers between Christians? If you do, for the sake of Christ's name, and for the health and unity of the church for which He shed His blood, I'd like to ask something of you: *Are you willing* to put your theology on the altar and allow the Spirit of God to heal, restore, and unite the body of Christ?

"Dear God, please tear down the walls and bring us together as *one*, so that the world may believe. Amen."

Chapter 7

Called to High Adventure: How to be Filled with the Holy Spirit

In the preceding chapters, I have presented a biblically based understanding of the gift of the Holy Spirit, I've addressed what it means to be baptized and filled with the Holy Spirit, and I've discussed the purpose and benefits of speaking in tongues. In this chapter, I want to answer another question: "*How* can I be filled with the Holy Spirit?" Knowing about the Holy Spirit and understanding what being filled with the Holy Spirit involves is one thing. Actually being filled with the Spirit is quite another. If one truly wants to experience the Spirit's fullness and to daily walk in that fullness, there are a number of important prerequisites or steps one may take. After reading these steps, you will find a prayer guide you can follow if you would like to pray for the Holy Spirit to fill you.

I know I run the risk here of being accused of oversimplifying the work of the Holy Spirit. As I said in Chapter 4, God is sovereign and He works in each of us in special and unique ways. Nevertheless, there are sound biblical principles, many of them already discussed, that are essential and basic to receiving and walking in the fullness of the Spirit. I believe, therefore, that we are safe in presenting them as general guidelines for every believer who wants more of God.

In Chapter 5, we identified six major areas of the Christian life that the Scriptures clearly link with the Spirit-filled life: Theses are: Spirit-filled Christians demonstrate an abiding state of spiritual growth and Christ-like character; Spirit-filled Christians are motivated and empowered to share their faith in Christ with others; Spirit-filled Christians are used as instruments of spiritual gifts that can come as an "inspiration of the moment;" Spirit-filled Christians fully participate in Christ-centered fellowship and body life; Spirit-filled Christians are inspired to praise and worship God; and Spirit-filled Christians have a growing compassion and anointing to minister to other people.

It is possible, and typical to a large degree, for believers to be spiritually "advanced" in some of the ways enumerated above but also to be spiritually stunted in other ways. Do you recall the wrapped packages in the Holy Spirit Gift Box? Some individuals routinely use supernatural spiritual gifts while having significant character flaws. But the opposite is also true. When it comes to demonstrating Christ-like character, some Christians are very much filled with the Spirit; yet they may be *clueless* when it comes to exercising supernatural gifts.

Some Christians are very powerful witnesses for Christ but have a long way to go in learning to worship God in Spirit and truth. Some may have attained great freedom of expression in worship but lack the Spirit's genuine passion for reaching the world for Christ or for ministering to other people.

Granted, our spiritual callings and gifts have something to do with our spiritual development and explain why some excel in ways that others do not. Still, in a general sense, every believer who genuinely wants to be filled with the Spirit should hunger for the Spirit's fullness in all these areas.

Should We Pray for More of the Holy Spirit?

By now, my conviction that we should desire and seek after the fullness of God's Spirit should be obvious. Some would argue that we don't need to ask for what we already have. Certainly, all true Christians do "have" the Holy Spirit. Nevertheless, having the Holy Spirit in my life does not necessarily mean that I am *filled* with the Holy Spirit. Let's use our Holy Spirit Gift Box analogy with the Gift Box containing a number of wrapped packages inside. We can say that we have received the gift of the Holy Spirit but that we have not unwrapped all the packages and appropriated their benefits in our life experience.

Someone might ask, "Okay, granted, by faith we need to appropriate all that God has given us in Christ and in the gift of the Holy Spirit. But does this mean we have to *ask* God for it?" I guess I don't really understand why some Christians make such a big deal about *asking* God for a fuller release of the Holy Spirit in their lives.

Perhaps part of the problem here is semantics. I really don't see much difference between praying that God will take possession of our lives totally, as some espouse, and praying that God will fill us, lead us, guide us, and empower us with His Spirit. When the disciples prayed in Acts 4:29–30 for empowerment to preach the gospel boldly and for healings and miraculous signs and wonders to accompany their preaching, what did they really want? It seems clear to me that they were asking for a fresh release of the Spirit's power and gifts. That is certainly what God *thought* they meant, because just look how He answered their prayers: "After they prayed, the place where they were meeting was shaken. And *they were all filled with the Holy Spirit and spoke the Word of God boldly*" (Acts 4:31).

It's important to note that being filled with the Spirit is not simply a one-time event. Yes, there is the initial reception of the Holy Spirit, and there are times of momentous breakthrough, as well as daily fillings with the Holy Spirit. These disciples had been filled on the Day of Pentecost and, facing persecution and challenges, needed to be filled again. Of course, we are no different in our need to be filled and refilled.

So, is it okay to pray for more of the Holy Spirit? Concerning the desirability of speaking in tongues, for example, one prominent evangelical leader espouses the position of "seek not; forbid not." This phrase sounds like King James Scripture. Unfortunately, however, only half of it is God's Word. Paul commands us concerning tongues in 1 Corinthians 14:39, "*Forbid not*" (KJV). Yet Scripture nowhere tells us, "Seek not the gift of tongues" (or any other gift of the Spirit, for that matter). Further, nowhere does Scripture instruct us to "seek the Giver, not the gift." Of course, we seek the Giver. But if we have pure motives, seeking gifts is not only permissible — it's good!

Paul exhorted the Corinthians to "eagerly desire spiritual gifts." It seems strange, then, to think Paul would command us to want something that he would expect us not to pray for. Sadly, the policy of "*seek not; forbid not*" cannot help but result in curbing or preventing a deeper and wider release of the Spirit's presence, power, gifts, and other workings in and through Christ's body.

Some have the attitude that "God has already gifted me to do certain things, so why would I insult Him by asking for another gift?" But I cannot imagine how in the world God would be insulted by our asking Him for more of His Spirit and gifts, enabling us to be even *more* effective in God's kingdom. God is far more insulted, I would think, by those who think they are so spiritually gifted that the Holy Spirit has nothing further to offer them. Of course, the final authority on whether we should pray for the Holy Spirit to fill us is our Lord Jesus Christ, who instructed his disciples:

> Ask and it will be given you; seek and you will find; knock and the door will be opened to you. For everyone who asks receives; he who seeks finds; and to him who knocks, the door will be opened. Which of you fathers, if your son asked for a fish, will give him a snake instead? Or if he asks for an egg, will give him a scorpion? If you then, though you are evil, know how to give good gifts to your children, how much more will your Father in heaven give the Holy Spirit to those who ***ask*** Him! (Luke 11:9–13)

Jesus presents us with a picture of God as a loving Father who delights in meeting the needs of His children. We all *need* to be filled with the Holy Spirit; indeed, His Word *commands* us to be filled. What could possibly be wrong with asking God to fill us with the

Holy Spirit? Nothing! This kind of prayer rejoices His heart because we pray it in accord with His will.

People, it is so important that we be Spirit-filled! Paul exhorts:

> Be very careful, then, how you live—not as unwise but as wise, making the most of every opportunity, because the days are evil. Therefore do not be foolish, but understand what the Lord's will is. Do not get drunk on wine, which leads to debauchery. *Instead, be filled with the Spirit.* (Ephesians 5:15–18)

These aren't just nice memory verses. God's Word projects an *urgency* about our being filled with the Spirit. "*The days are evil,*" the needs are great, the gospel must be proclaimed, and we cannot do what God needs us to do without being filled with the Holy Spirit. We cannot afford to settle for less in these urgent times. Just listen to what some of God's choice servants have had to say about this:

- Andrew Murray underscored how vital this subject is when he wrote that people, "ought to seek with their whole hearts to be filled with the Spirit of God. Without being filled with the Spirit it is utterly impossible that an individual Christian or a church could ever live or work as God desires."
- One of America's most outstanding Christian leaders and evangelists, Charles Finney wrote in the 1800's, "Christians are as guilty for not being filled with His Holy Spirit as sinners are for not repenting. They are even more so, for as they have more light they are so much the more guilty."
- The great Henrietta Mears wrote, "I believe that it is impossible for any Christian to be effective either in his life or in his service unless he is filled with the Holy Spirit — who is God's only provision of power."
- Bill Bright urged: "Every Christian not only has the prerogative of being filled with the Holy Spirit, but is also admonished to be filled with the Holy Spirit. Therefore if a Christian is not filled he is disobedient to the command of

> God, who commands us to be filled, and is sinning against Him. Further, since God commands us in His Word to be filled with the Spirit, we may be certain that He has the power to fill us the very moment we invite Him to do so."[26]

Because God's Word commands us to be filled with the Holy Spirit, every believer has an *obligation* to be filled. Therefore, if for some reason we choose to prevent the Holy Spirit from filling us, I believe God will hold us accountable. Yes, I believe that we are *accountable to God* for all the ministry we could have done and all the lives we could have touched had we sought more of the Holy Spirit. Therefore, let's now look at key steps for being filled with the Spirit.

Steps to Being Filled with the Holy Spirit

Step 1: Make a Decision to Receive Jesus Christ as Savior and Lord

This step is obvious: Unless we are Christians, the Holy Spirit will not fill us. If you have never received Jesus Christ into your life, that is where to begin. On the Day of Pentecost, Peter instructed his hearers to "*repent* and *be baptized* . . . in the name of Jesus Christ, and *you will receive the gift of the Holy Spirit*." Repentance involves turning from a self-centered life and turning to Christ, making *Him* the center of your life. It involves turning away from sins and receiving Christ's forgiveness and cleansing. If you have never received Christ, I invite you to pray the following prayer (or your own adaptation of this prayer) expressing your desire to receive Christ:

---

[26] Quotes taken from Bill Bright, *The Coming Revival: America's Call to Fast, Pray, and Seek God's Face* (Orlando: New Life Publications, 1995), 195-196.

Dear Father in heaven, thank you for your love for me. Thank you that you sent your Son Jesus Christ to die for my sins. I now turn from self-centeredness and sin and invite Jesus into my heart to be my Savior and Lord. Please come into my heart, Lord Jesus. Thank you that you forgive all my sins and welcome me into your family as your own child. Thank you that I am born-again. Help me to live for you. Amen.

Christ assures us that if we sincerely receive Him, He does come into our lives (see John 1:12; Revelation 3:20). If you sincerely prayed to receive Him, you can be assured that He has heard your prayer and that He has come into your life. WELCOME to God's family! "If anyone is in Christ, he is a new creation; the old has gone, the new has come!" (2 Corinthian 5:17). Praise the Lord!

Step 2: Awaken or Develop a Desire to Be Filled with the Holy Spirit

Do you remember the oil refinery story I told you earlier? (See "There's More" in Chapter 4). Those who have no desire for more of the Holy Spirit will rarely receive more. Those who "hunger and thirst" after God and His righteousness are the ones who "will be filled" (Matthew 5:6). If you are not aware of a desire for more in your life, confess it to the Lord, and ask Him to increase your hunger for him.

It is also very important to examine our *motives* for wanting more. Remember that God doesn't fill us with His Spirit to make us feel good or to provide us with ecstatic spiritual experiences. He doesn't give Him to make us look good or to give us a big name in the body of Christ. Rather, He gives His Spirit so we will be more like Jesus, exalting *Him* and making *Him* look good.

Of course, the Holy Spirit *does bless us.* He gives us peace and joy and fills our lives with God's love. Still, if our main purpose in seeking the Holy Spirit is our own blessing, our motives are not what they should be. Here are the purest motives for wanting the Holy

Spirit to fill us: To glorify God and exalt His Son, Jesus Christ; and, to bear fruit for Christ, allowing Him to do His ministry through us by the Holy Spirit's power and anointing.

If we want to make a significant impact in this world for God's glory, our hearts must burn with passion for Christ. Jesus said, "Let your light shine before men, that they may see your good deeds and praise your Father in heaven" (Matthew 5:16).

Take some time now to examine your motives for wanting more of the Holy Spirit in your life. Confess to the Lord any impure or self-seeking motives and receive by faith His forgiveness and cleansing (see 1 John 1:9). Ask Him to give you right and pure motives—an earnest desire to honor and serve Him effectively and to give Him all the glory. If you feel no real desire for more of the Holy Spirit in your life, confess that to the Lord, and ask Him to change your heart, filling you with that desire.

Step 3: Prepare Yourself for Spiritual Warfare

As a believer who wants to be filled with the Holy Spirit, you threaten Satan and his plans for retaining and expanding his kingdom of darkness. You can expect that he and his demonic cohorts intend to target you for attack. John the Baptist baptized Jesus, God's Spirit descended upon Him like a dove, and the Father spoke from heaven, "This is my Son, whom I love; with him I am well pleased" (see Matthew 3:13–17). Is it any wonder that in the very next verse Jesus is found in the desert, where He endured forty days of intense spiritual testing and attack?

As you step out in faith to be filled with the Holy Spirit, be sure to prepare yourself for the resistance that may confront you. The apostle Peter writes: "Be self-controlled and alert. Your enemy the devil prowls around like a roaring lion looking for someone to devour. Resist him, standing firm in the faith . . ." (1 Peter 5:8–9).

The devil assaults our minds, our bodies, our emotions, our very faith. He wants to hinder us, to oppress us, and to in every way possible destroy our witness for Christ. He uses deceptions, demonic oppression, blasphemous impulses and thoughts, accusations, temptations of sensual pleasure, feelings of separation, and even other believers to intimidate and condemn us, and prevent us from serving God. This dangerous enemy seeks "to steal and kill and destroy" (John 10:10); but we should not let him intimidate us. Jesus came through His time of testing armed with great power and authority. The following scriptures attest to the fact that our Lord Jesus Christ gives us victory, too:

- I have given you authority to trample on snakes and scorpions and to overcome all the power of the enemy; nothing will harm you. (Luke 10:19)
- You, dear children, are from God and have overcome them, because the one who is in you is greater than the one who is in the world. (1 John 4:4)
- For the accuser of our brothers, who accuses them before our God day and night, has been hurled down. They overcame him by the blood of the Lamb and by the word of their testimony . . . (Revelation 12:10–11)
- No weapon forged against you will prevail, and you will refute every tongue that accuses you. This is the heritage of the servants of the Lord, and this is their vindication from me, declares the Lord. (Isaiah 54:17)

When we resist the devil in the name of Jesus Christ and by the power of His sinless blood, he must flee. Nevertheless, we must take this formidable enemy seriously and arm ourselves for spiritual combat. Meditate, personalize, and pray through these vitally important exhortations from the apostle Paul:

> Finally, be strong in the Lord and in his mighty power. Put on the full armor of God so that you can take your stand against the devil's schemes. For our struggle is not against flesh and blood, but against the rulers, against the authori-

> ties, against the powers of this dark world and against the spiritual forces of evil in the heavenly realms. Therefore put on the full armor of God, so that when the day of evil comes, you may be able to stand your ground, and after you have done everything, to stand. (Ephesians 6:10–13)

Jesus defeated Satan's attacks during His forty days of wilderness testing (see Matthew 4:1–11). Each time the devil tempted Him, He used Scripture as His spiritual sword. Overcoming each lie and deception, He proclaimed, "*It is written* . . ."! Let us also press into the victory that is ours through Jesus Christ!

Step 4: Deal with Past and Present Sins

We must remember that the Spirit of God is the *HOLY* Spirit. We cannot expect Him to fill us if we knowingly and willfully involve ourselves in sinful behaviors. Paul the apostle urges us, "Do not grieve the Holy Spirit with whom you were sealed for the day of redemption" (Ephesians 4:30). Paul discusses specific sins in Ephesians 4:17–5:5, all of which grieve the Holy Spirit: giving oneself over to sensuality, impurity, and lust (4:19); falsehood (4:25); anger (4:26); stealing (4:28); unwholesome talk (4:29); bitterness, rage, and anger (4:31); brawling, slander, and malice (4:31); sexual immorality and impurity (5:3, 5); greed (5:3, 5); and obscenity, foolish talk, and coarse joking (5:4).

Paul exhorts God's people to turn away from these sins, "for because of such things God's wrath comes on those who are disobedient" (5:6). He reminds us to "put off your old self, which is being corrupted by its deceitful desires" and "to put on the new self, created to be like God in true righteousness and holiness" (4:22–24). "For you were once darkness," he says, "but now you are light in the Lord. Live as children of light (for the fruit of the light consists in all goodness, righteousness and truth) and find out what pleases the Lord. Have nothing to do with the fruitless deeds of darkness, but rather expose them" (5:8–11).

We all have sin in our lives. We do not have to be perfect in order to be filled with the Spirit, but we do need to have an earnest desire to be freed from sin. Through the blood of Jesus Christ we can be free, not only from the *guilt* of sin (God forgives us and reconciles us to Himself through Christ) but also from the *power* of sin. We must openly acknowledge and confess our sins to God (see 1 John 1:9), and at times to one another (see James 5:16), renouncing those sins in Jesus' name. In doing so, we can trust Christ to cleanse us and give us victory. As the apostle John wrote, "If we walk in the light as he (God) is in the light, we have fellowship with one another and the blood of Jesus, his Son, purifies us from all sin" (1 John 1:7).

Are you currently entangled in a sinful behavior or relationship? Do you harbor some kind of secret sin? Or maybe you are simply so busy that you have crowded out the Holy Spirit's life. Whatever the problem, you must deal with it sincerely, honestly and firmly. Repent! Turn away from it. Not only does it prevent you from being filled with the Spirit—your sin will effectually grieve and quench the Spirit's presence right out of your life.

Ordinarily, you can take care of these impediments directly between you and God, unless you have sinned with or against another person or persons. In this case, you will need to confess your sin to the person(s) involved, ask for forgiveness, and in instances where possible, make things right.

At other times, a particular sin may keep you bound. Let's say, for example, that a lustful craving for pornography grips you. You go to God directly, but you find no release. Then you need to follow the directives of James 5:16: *"Therefore confess your sins to each other and pray for each other so that you may be healed.*" We definitely need help sometimes, especially when we're losing the battle to the sin nature and Satan. Confession to a couple of trusted brothers or sisters in Christ humbles us, but "God gives grace to the humble." I have seen many people set free from sinful bondages simply by obeying this command of Scripture. (For more on being freed from habitual sin and other related problems, see *Appendix B: Freedom from Handles of the Enemy.)*

In saying this, I do not suggest that we must be completely free and whole in every area of our lives before the Holy Spirit can fill us. Yet, before we can deeply experience the Holy Spirit's fullness in our lives, we must deal with certain key problem areas of past and present sin in preparation for a deeper filling of the Holy Spirit in our lives.

Step 5: Surrender Completely to the Lordship of Jesus

Self-will is one of the greatest obstacles to being filled with the Holy Spirit. How can the Holy Spirit lead us if we insist on controlling everything ourselves? A man may wade out in a river until he is in water up to his waist, or even to his neck. Yet as long as he has his feet on the bottom, he is not moving with the current. He still controls his situation. Once he gets in over his head, however, and his feet leave the bottom, he can be led by the river's current. Likewise, a person may have the Holy Spirit in his life. He may be in the Spirit up to his waist or neck, but until he releases the reins of his life to Jesus Christ, fully and completely, God's Spirit cannot fill him. Paul the apostle wrote: "I appeal to you therefore, brothers and sisters, by the mercies of God, to present your bodies as a living sacrifice, holy and acceptable to God, which is your spiritual worship" (Romans 12:1, NRSV).

In the Old Testament, the Jewish people offered sacrifices to God. They gave the priests animals to present on the altar to atone for their sins. The fire of God consumed them. But Christ fulfilled the Old Testament law of sacrifice once and for all when He died on the cross for our sins. Thus, John the Baptist's cry: "Look, the Lamb of God who takes away the sin of the world" (John 1:29). In the New Testament, we no longer offer sacrifices for our sins. Christ accomplished a complete and final atonement for our sins. Our appropriate response to what He has done is to *offer ourselves* as living sacrifices to God. We have *died* to our self-will, our selfish ambition, our self-centered priorities, and now we will *live* for Christ. As fire engulfed the sacrifices in the Old Testament, so the Holy Spirit engulfs us, the *living sacrifice*, enabling us to live fully for Christ.

How important is it that we understand this? Very. God gives the Holy Spirit to those who *obey* Him (see Acts 5:32). Years ago, a group of ministers met together to consider inviting an evangelist to their city for a crusade. As they shared their ideas, one man suggested Dwight L. Moody, a truly anointed and consecrated man of God whom God used to bring a *million* souls to Christ. (And this was *before* TV. and airplanes!) Someone interjected, "Why does everyone think so highly of D. L. Moody? Does he have a monopoly on the Holy Spirit?" The swift reply was, "No; but the Holy Spirit has a monopoly on him!"

That's what needs to happen in us. Just think what the Holy Spirit could do through us if He had a monopoly! How can we give Him a monopoly? By taking the risk and surrendering our entire lives to Christ, putting Him first and making Him Lord of every area of our lives. I often pray this prayer: "Lord, all I am, all I have, and all I can do—I give to You."

Jesus Christ is Sovereign Lord of the universe! But He is a "Gentleman." He doesn't coerce us to bow our knee to Him (not yet, anyway–but He will some day (see Philippians 2:5–11)! Sometimes He "turns up the heat," to make us aware of the stubborn self-will in certain areas of our lives. Nevertheless, it is up to us to make the conscious and deliberate surrender of our lives to His Lordship. Unless and until we do that, we can never, repeat *NEVER,* be filled with the Holy Spirit.

Before I became a Christian, I was an independent, self-willed person. I well remember one of my Davidson College psych classes. My professor had asked us to share what animal we would be if we had to be one. "I'd be a wild black stallion," I bragged, "running free with the wind, answerable to *no one*." Then I became a Christian. God used some painful experiences to teach me valuable lessons. I learned that my wild stallion life wasn't so free, after all. In fact, my life had no true meaning or purpose until I met the Master and let him break and harness me with bit and bridle. Only then could the Master use and direct my life in the one truly *great* adventure.

Prayerfully examine your life. Ask God to show you any areas where you resist His leadership and control. Confess and repent of any self-will and stubbornness He shows you. Firmly decide to surrender every area of your life to Him. Give Him yourself, your family, friends, romantic relationships, time, job, money, home, cars, interests, pursuits, pleasures, past, present, and future—everything. Tell Him, in the words of the old hymn, "I surrender all, I surrender all; all to Thee, my blessed Savior, I surrender all."

Step 6: Be Awakened to Who You Are in Christ and to What He Has Given You

Let me tell you the story of a man from one of the small Baltic States. This man desperately wanted to come to America, the land of freedom and opportunity. Over several years he saved enough money to purchase a ticket on a large ocean liner to take him the entire distance from Europe to the New York Harbor. Since it took all his money just to purchase the ticket, he knew he didn't have enough to buy any of the ship's food. So he loaded up with cheese and crackers.

The man felt grateful and excited for his voyage to freedom. Nevertheless, walking past the dining rooms at meal times and seeing gleeful people feasting sumptuously was hard for him to take. Oh, the luscious aromas of the meats, the huge tables filled with fruits, vegetables, breads and pastries. It was unbearable! So at meal times the man made it a point to stay in his cabin and "dine in." He'd pull out his Spartan little meal of cheese and crackers and tell himself, "'Tis a small price to pay for a new life in America."

Finally, the exciting day came when the ship sailed into New York Harbor. The man's spirit soared as he saw the Statue of Liberty on Ellis Island, and his heart overflowed with thanksgiving for safe passage to the land of opportunity. As the ship prepared to dock, our friend stood with his bags, eager to disembark. A ship steward approached and warmly said, "We certainly hope you enjoyed your journey with us." The man grinned and replied, "I can't tell you how thankful I am to be here. The trip was wonderful!" Then he added, "You know, the only thing that was hard on me was that I couldn't afford the food onboard. While others were eating the buffet meals, I had to settle for cheese and crackers in my cabin."

"No! You can't be serious!" exclaimed the steward. "Didn't you know that the price of your ticket included all the food you could eat!?"

Ouch! Doesn't that hurt? But aren't so many of us just like this man? We are so grateful to be saved and on our way to heaven, so appreciative for forgiveness and eternal life, that we dare not think there could be more for us. God has given us many more blessings in Christ, but our limited paradigm won't allow us to expect them!

Paul the apostle wrote, "Praise be to the God and Father of our Lord Jesus Christ, who has blessed us in the heavenly realms with every spiritual blessing in Christ" (Ephesians 1:3). Christ "bought our ticket," and the price He paid covers *every spiritual blessing* in Him. If we ever hope to walk in the fullness of God's Spirit, we've got to grasp this *amazing* truth. Remember, Jesus said, "Then you will know the truth, and the truth will set you free" (John 8:32).

So often our understanding of what God wants to give us and how He wants to bless us is woefully inadequate. Thus, we pray woefully inadequate, anemic prayers with little if any expectation. Why do we do this to ourselves? Perhaps because somewhere in our hearts we believe God blesses us according to what *we deserve* rather than according to "his glorious riches in Christ Jesus" (Philippians 4:19).

It is true that our sins can quench and grieve away the Holy Spirit's presence. But many of us approach God with very little expectation of blessing or victory, even after we have confessed and repented of every sin and God has forgiven us. We need to realize that when we put our faith in Christ, God imputes the righteousness of His Son Jesus Christ to us. He accepts us and loves us and blesses us *on the basis of* ***Christ's*** *merits,* not our own.

Listen again as Paul exhorts the Ephesians to wake up and "see" what God has already given them because of their faith in Christ:

> I pray also that the eyes of your heart may be enlightened in order that you may know the hope to which he has called you, the riches of his glorious inheritance in the saints, and his incomparably great power for us who believe. That power is like the working of his mighty strength, which he exerted in Christ when he raised him from the dead and seated him at his right hand in the heavenly realms.
> (Ephesians 1:18–20).

God wants to awaken *us* to all He has given us in Christ. He wants us to know the hope, the glorious inheritance, and the *incomparably great power* available to us who believe in Him. Consider this: the power of God that raised Jesus Christ from the dead, *the resurrection power of the Holy Spirit*, is available to us now—yes, *now*!—because we believe in Christ.

Notice in this passage where Christ is seated. He died on the cross, but God the Father "raised Him from the dead and *seated* Him at His right hand in the heavenly realms." The New Testament tells us repeatedly that Jesus Christ presently sits at *the right hand* of God the Father. Here is a sampling of these scriptures:

- After the Lord Jesus had spoken to them, he was taken up into heaven and he sat at the *right hand of God.* (Mark 16:19)
- Exalted to the r*ight hand of God*, he has received from the Father the promised Holy Spirit and has poured out what you now see and hear. (Acts 2:33)
- God exalted him to his own *right hand* as Prince and Savior that he might give repentance and forgiveness of sins to Israel. (Acts 5:31)

- But Stephen, full of the Holy Spirit, looked up to heaven and saw the glory of God, and Jesus standing *at the right hand of God.* "Look," he said, "I see heaven open and the Son of Man standing at the *right hand of God.*" (Acts 7:55–56)
- Christ Jesus, who died—more than that, who was raised to life—is at the *right hand of God* and is also interceding for us. (Romans 8:34)
- Jesus Christ, who has gone into heaven and is at *God's right hand*—with angels, authorities, and powers in submission to him. (1 Peter 3:21–22)

God's right hand is the place of honor, power, authority, and victory. Christ rose from the dead and sits at His Father's right hand, where He has immediate access to His Father. From this exalted position He intercedes for us and exercises authority over all principalities, powers, and authorities. He is the Champion, the Victor. And by faith we share in His victory.

But there is more! Read this next page or two carefully. The biblical truth I am about to present has the power to change your life *forever.* Jesus, as we have already seen, sits at the right hand of the Father in heaven. Now let's see where *we* are in relationship to Him. Paul tells us in Ephesians 2:1–3 that prior to our being saved we were spiritually dead, following the world and the devil, bound by our sin nature and doomed to face God's judgment. That's the bad news; but now listen to the good news. He says: "But because of his great love for us, God, who is rich in mercy, made *us* alive with Christ . . . And God raised *us* up with Christ and seated *us* with him in the heavenly realms in Christ Jesus" (Ephesians 2:4–7).

Let this astounding truth sink in. God's Word says that not only is Christ seated at God's right hand, but that *we, too, are seated with Christ* at God's right hand. Through our faith in Christ, God has raised us up and seated us with Christ at the place of tremendous blessing, honor, power, authority, and victory. Clearly, we do not deserve to be there by our own merit, but because of Christ's merits we are there just the same.

God brought this wonderful truth home to me years ago. My grandmother, Mama Lucy, was ill, and my dad called to tell me I should come see her in Virginia before she passed away. I made an airline reservation to fly from Los Angeles to see her. Cheri, along with our children, saw me off at the Continental Airlines gate. As I waited in line, I recognized a former presidential candidate, John B. Anderson, getting on the plane. When I arrived at the check-in counter, the ticket agent said, "Mr. Ford, we don't seem to have you on our computer. You'll have to wait to see if there are any seats left." I waited and waited. Finally, she called me up and informed me that only one open seat remained on the entire plane. "It's First Class—is that okay?" she asked. Since I had paid only $258 for my round-trip ticket, I had no trouble deciding. "Sure, that will be fine!" Needless to say, I was thrilled.

As I boarded the plane, I saw the only available seat right beside none other than John B. Anderson. We talked across the entire country. I shared my faith in Christ with him and took him to task for his views on several issues important to me (I'm sure he was never happier to get off a plane in his entire life!). I learned something about air travel I had never known before about air travel—flying first class is a great way to fly! Oh, how I relished those first class extras—plenty of leg room (I'm 6'3"), very comfortable seats, a choice of filet mignon or chicken cordon bleu for dinner, freshly ground pepper on my freshly tossed salad, a hot towel to wipe my brow. . . My, my, my!

After visiting and praying with Mama Lucy, I returned to California. Three weeks later she went to be with Jesus. Again, I called my travel agent and somehow secured another round-trip ticket on Continental Airlines for $258.00. I went up to the ticket counter halfway expecting to hear that they had no seat for me. But to my pleasant surprise the agent gave me a boarding pass and seat assignment.

Coincidentally, a good friend named Joe, was on the same flight. We liked to kid around, laughing and joking together. When it came time to board the plane, Joe went right to his seat. When I got to my seat, however, a young woman was sitting in it. I showed her my ticket. "I believe you're in my seat," I said. She got out her ticket. Lo and behold, we had been assigned the same seat!

Aware of our predicament, Joe laughed at me as I explained our problem to our flight attendant. "Clay's not going to get a seat," he sang teasingly. The flight attendant asked me to wait at the back of the plane until all other passengers had taken their seats. Joe kept up his ribbing as the entire coach section filled up.

"It looks like there are no seats left" the flight attendant reported to me. "Well, that's OK," I said with a grin. "I don't mind sitting in First Class." She said, "Follow me," and then she escorted me through the coach section on up to First Class and into a delightfully soft and spacious seat.

Quite large in those days, Joe found coach seats most uncomfortable. And at my size, I, too, have never relished coach seats. When Joe saw the flight attendant seating me in First Class, he nearly had a fit! I leaned out in the aisle and looked back to him and grinned broadly. He shook his fist and mouthed, "Get *me* up there!" Shrugging my shoulders and smiling nonchalantly, I said, "Gee, Joe, I wish I could do something to help you." He and I had many laughs over this incident in subsequent years. (Now Joe is in heaven—no better seats anywhere!)

This time I sat beside Ted Mann, the owner of the Mann movie theater chain. We had a wonderful time together. I said to him: "You know, Mr. Ted Mann. I don't really deserve to be here. I only paid $258 round trip for this ticket. But God put me here in First Class right beside you, because He wanted me to tell you how much He loves you." His eyes welled up with tears, and he replied, "You know . . . I've always felt like there's Someone up there looking after me." No doubt his lovely Christian wife, actress Rhonda Fleming, had prayed for such encounters.

Now why do I tell you this story? In these travel experiences God drove home a great truth to me: I didn't deserve my seat in First

Class. While a typical First Class fare might run $1,000-1,500, I paid a mere $258! But that didn't matter—*I was seated in First Class, and because I was, I enjoyed all the blessings, rights and privileges* given to First Class passengers.

Similarly, we Christians are seated with Christ at God's right hand. We don't at all deserve that position—we certainly didn't pay for the "ticket" nor could we ever earn it or afford it. In fact, we did nothing whatsoever to deserve it. Jesus Christ paid the full price for our seat at the Cross of Calvary so He could offer it as a *free gift*. And because we are seated there, we receive all the blessings, rights, and privileges given in Him!

Just think! All the *blessings*: the fullness of his grace and mercy, forgiveness of sin, healing, reconciliation with God, peace, love, joy, eternal life, the promise of heaven; the Holy Spirit's presence, life, power, gifts, and fruit . . . All the *rights and privileges*: victory over Satan, sin, and death; the right as God's child to immediate access to our wonderful, loving, awesome, almighty, Heavenly Father any time, day or night.

Now back to my story, what if I had sniveled to the flight attendant that I didn't deserve first class and insisted that I stay in coach? That would have been silly, even foolish, wouldn't it? But that's exactly what many of us do when we allow our own sense of guilt, unworthiness, and false-humility—whatever!—to hold us back from receiving the wonderful gifts of grace that God wants to give us. God offers us liberation, the opportunity and high privilege to sit with Christ and reign with Him and to boldly take hold of His blessings. We serve Him and our own destiny best by taking the seat Christ has provided us, at the right hand of our Father in heaven.

In seeking God for the fullness of His Spirit, our level of expectancy and faith is greatly enhanced when we come to this understanding of who we are in Christ and what we have been given in Him. This amazing truth, if you can grasp it, will change your life forever.

Step 7: Ask in Prayer, Believing That You Will Receive

We have already discussed earlier in this chapter why asking God to fill us with the Holy Spirit is absolutely appropriate. "How much more," Jesus said, "will the Father give the Holy Spirit to those who *ask* Him" (Luke 11:13). James wrote, "You do not have, because you do not ask God" (James 4:2). This verse's context does not specifically relate to asking God for His Spirit. However, this statement is true in the general sense that we should ask God for anything we need, which would include the Holy Spirit.

Jesus taught us to pray, "Give us today our daily bread" (Matthew 6:11). God knows we have daily needs, and He could meet our needs without our asking. Yet Jesus instructs us to ask Him just the same. Doing this reminds us that we have a Father who loves us; that our provision comes not by our own hand, but by the One we trust and rely upon for everything. The act of asking our Father to meet our needs keeps us humble before Him and also before others. It fosters a joyous spirit of thanksgiving and praise to Him as He faithfully answers our prayers.

Reading Deuteronomy 8 reminds us of our total dependence on God:

> When you have eaten and are satisfied, praise the Lord your God for the good land he has given you. Be careful that you do not forget the Lord your God, failing to observe his commands, his laws and his decrees that I am giving you this day. Otherwise, when you eat and are satisfied, when you build fine houses and settle down, and when your herds and flocks grow large and your silver and gold increase and all you have is multiplied, then your heart will become proud and you will forget the Lord your God, who brought you out of Egypt, out of the land of slavery. He led you through the vast and dreadful desert, that thirsty and waterless land, with its venomous snakes and scorpions. He brought you water out of hard rock. He gave you manna to eat in the desert, something your fathers had never known, to humble and to test you so that in the end it might go well

> with you. You may say to yourself, 'My power and the strength of my hands have produced this wealth for me.' But remember the Lord your God, for it is he who gives you the ability to produce wealth. (Deuteronomy 8:10–18)

As I have reflected on the numerous and great blessings that God has bestowed upon my family, my heart overflows with love and thanksgiving toward God. Once I wrote in the margin of one of my study bibles this response to what I read in verses 10–18:

> When God has blessed you and caused you to prosper, never forget that *He* is the One who has blessed you. It is not *your* doing but His. Don't let your heart become proud; don't ever forget the blessings and miracles that God has done in your life. Never take Him for granted; always remember to love Him, thank Him, bless Him, obey Him, revere Him, honor Him, serve Him. Remember that *God* is the One who gives you the ability to produce wealth. Don't ever allow your heart to stray from loving Him or your will from obeying Him.

I believe this is how God wants our hearts to respond to Him. That is why acknowledging our needs and humbly asking Him to meet them is right and good. When it comes to wanting to be filled with the Holy Spirit, the most natural and appropriate thing to do is to approach our Father in prayer. We can ask Him, humbly yet very expectantly, to meet this need in our lives.

Yes, God wants us to pray expectantly, filled with faith and assurance that He will hear our prayer and answer it according to His will. We already know that God wills for us to be filled with the Holy Spirit. As we have seen, He *commands* us to be filled (Ephesians 5:18), so it *must be* His will. And God's Word assures us that He will answer our prayers when we pray according to His will:

> This is the confidence we have in approaching God: that if we ask anything according to His will, he hears us. And if

> we know that He hears us—whatever we ask—we know that we have what we have asked of Him. (1 John 5:14–15).

Faith and expectancy are very important as we pray for the fullness of the Holy Spirit. We know that "without faith it is impossible to please God," and that "anyone who comes to him must believe that he exists and that he rewards those who earnestly seek him*"* (Hebrews 11:6). Don't we receive Christ by faith, trusting that He hears us when we invite Him into our lives? Similarly, we ask in faith for the Holy Spirit to fill us to overflowing, to release His power, gifts, fruit, and other workings ever increasingly in our lives. Jesus taught us something very remarkable about faith. He said:

> "Have faith in God," Jesus answered. "I tell you the truth, if anyone says to this mountain, `Go, throw yourself into the sea,' and does not doubt in his heart but believes that what he says will happen, it will be done for him. Therefore I tell you, *whatever you ask for in prayer, believe that you have received it, and it will be yours."* (Mark 11:22–24)

Pray humbly. Pray boldly and expectantly, trusting that God has heard your prayer and that His answer is on the way.

Step 8: Receive Thankfully, and Then Step Out in Faith and Obedience

We come now to the final step: gratefully receiving the Holy Spirit's fullness and then stepping out in the assurance of this reality to obey and serve God. As we go through these steps in earnest, we can take Him at His Word, that He will answer our prayer because He wills to do it. Remember that you are not dictating to God. He is no spiritual "vending machine" you can coerce into doing your bidding. He is not some law or ideal principle or technique that you learn to manage and manipulate. He is your heavenly Father—a PERSON, one who loves you and wants to bless and use your life in service of

Jesus. Receive His fullness by faith, thanking Him for all He has done, is doing, and will do in and through your life.

A thankful heart is precious to God and central to our lives as Christians. Thankfulness is one of the highest expressions of faith because it demonstrates confidence that God will indeed answer your prayers. Paul encourages us:

> Rejoice! Let your gentleness be evident to all. The Lord is near. Do not be anxious about anything, but in everything, by prayer and petition, with *thanksgiving*, present your requests to God. And the peace of God, which transcends all understanding, will guard your hearts and your minds in Christ Jesus. (Philippians 4:4–7)

Thank Him and praise Him for filling you. He is worthy! He is awesome! Ask Him for help as you open the packages in your Holy Spirit Gift Box that you have left unwrapped or not yet fully received or experienced: the Spirit's love for the lost, the power to witness, freedom to praise, gifts to serve, growth into Christ-like character, full participation in His body . . . Ask Him to light a fire in your intercessory prayer life, and ask Him to speak to you in His Word. Ask Him to fill you to overflowing that you may exalt Christ and make Him known, that you may bear fruit and glorify Him . . . Surrender unreservedly, open yourself completely, and gratefully receive His fullness. Keep praising and thanking Him, and as the Spirit leads you, feel free to step out in faith to praise Him in tongues. Speak out whatever words He gives you in praise, thanksgiving, and adoration of your Lord. Trust that He has filled you.

Finally, as you have received this fresh filling of the Spirit—perhaps a major new release, a momentous breakthrough for you—remember that God fills you for a purpose. He will continue to fill you as you give away what you have received from Him. Step out in faith to do all the Holy Spirit inspires and enables you to do. Don't hold back; go for it! Jump into the flow of ministry. Remember, a stream that continually gives itself away stays fresh and alive; a pond that gives nothing away becomes stagnant and filled with slime. Also, remember you reap what you sow. "Give," Jesus said, "and it will be given to you. A good measure, pressed down, shaken together and running over, will be poured into your lap. For with the measure you use, it will be measured to you." (Luke 6:38)

So give of yourself. Use your gifts to honor God and serve His church. Let His light shine through you to a lost and needy world. Give generously and sacrificially to His work—both your time and your financial resources. Know that "God *loves* a cheerful giver" and that "whoever sows generously will also reap generously." (see 2 Corinthians 9:6). Decide that God will use your life, His Spirit working mightily in and through you, to make an impact in your world for Jesus Christ. Then, praise Him and thank Him some more!

Praying Through the Steps

If you would like the Holy Spirit to fill you, you can either pray through these steps by yourself or with others. Go to a quiet place free of distractions, and allow enough time to pray through these steps in a meaningful way. Spend some time meditating on God's word, praying, and praising Him until you become aware that you are in His presence. Then pray through these eight steps as outlined or as you feel led. Although it may not be necessary, I believe praying through these steps aloud can be quite helpful. It might help to go back over this chapter and jot down specific things to pray about in each step.

Step One: Commit yourself to Jesus Christ. Invite Him into your life if you have not done so before, trusting Him to be your Lord and Savior. Thank Him for living in your heart.

Step Two: Express your desire to be filled with the Holy Spirit. Confess any impure motives and ask God to give you a heart that wants more of Him so that you can serve Christ more powerfully for His glory. We should be like "the deer panting after running streams," earnestly desiring God's living water.

Step Three: Prepare yourself for spiritual warfare. Prayerfully put on the full armor of God described in Ephesians 6:12–18, and resolve that you will be victorious in Jesus' name over every enemy attack.

Step Four: Turn away from your sins, renouncing them aloud as an act of your will. Break free from Satan's handles on your life by renouncing past and present sins and any demonic handles attached to them. Renounce these sins forcefully, in the name of Jesus Christ. Deal particularly with areas of habitual sin, unforgiveness, and any past or present involvement in the occult.

Step Five: Surrender yourself completely to Jesus Christ. Put Him first in your life, and ask Him to exercise His Lordship in every area of your life.

Step Six: Ask God to awaken your understanding to know who you are in Christ and what He has given you in Christ. Thank Him that you are seated with Christ at God's right hand and for the victory and authority over sin and Satan you have in Christ.

Step Seven: Ask God to fill you with His Holy Spirit. Pray boldly and expectantly, believing that you will receive because you are praying according to His will.

Step Eight: Receive the Holy Spirit's release and fullness by faith and with great praise and thanksgiving to God. Decide that as you receive you will step out in faith and wholehearted obedience to do all He leads you to do.

Praise the Lord! If you have prayed through these steps, trust that God has answered your prayer; then act on it in faith. Don't wait for an emotional experience to confirm that He has filled you. Emotions and dramatic spiritual experiences may or may not accompany the answer to your prayer. Remember, Jesus said, "Whatever you ask for in prayer, believe that you *have received* it, and it *will be* yours" (Mark 11:24). Don't let unbelief rob you. Remember, this is warfare. Praise the Lord, and keep praising Him for filling you. Then, ask God how He would have you serve Him. Step out in faith and minister in the Spirit's power for God's glory.

Don't concern yourself at this point over whether or not you have an emotional experience. That is a peripheral issue that doesn't really matter. What matters is that you begin in faith to give away what God has given you by investing it in ministry and service to others. You will subsequently find that your gifts and anointing will grow and deepen, and you will enjoy an ever-enriching journey with the Holy Spirit.

One final thought: Praying through these steps is not a once-for-all-time event. Let me encourage you to pray through these steps often for a fresh filling, whenever you feel the need to be refreshed in the Spirit. At times God may grant momentous breakthroughs and dramatic fillings in your life. Regardless, whether they are major and dramatic, or not, we should always be filled with the Holy Spirit. Remember, as you live this Spirit-filled life, be sure to give Him all the glory for what He does, praying, "***Yours*** *is the kingdom and the power and the glory forever. Amen and Amen!* God bless you!

Appendix A

"Rightly Dividing the Word of Truth"

Before we can adequately discuss theological topics such as "the baptism of the Holy Spirit" and speaking in tongues, we must adopt some ground rules for properly interpreting the Scriptures. As an evangelical Christian, I am thoroughly committed to the authority of the Scriptures as our infallible guide to both doctrinal truth and practical Christian living. If we don't acknowledge the Scriptures as the final authority in all areas, then we begin with different presuppositions and commitments that make our coming together in understanding very difficult if not impossible.

I thankfully realize, however, that almost all evangelical Christians acknowledge the authority of the Scriptures, and, with that in common, we are more than halfway there. Many of our difficulties concerning the Holy Spirit's ministry are caused by different methods or practices we use to interpret the Bible. I do not regard myself as an eminent scholar, nor do most of you, I assume, who are reading this book. (However I have done my share of studying and teaching on the fundamentals of biblical interpretation.) I encourage students of the Word to study books like *Reading the Bible for All It's Worth* by Gordon Fee and Douglas Stuart. This can be immensely helpful in our quest to interpret the Bible more accurately and responsibly.

More than a few times I've heard someone smugly say, "I think we should just let the Bible speak for itself." That can sound so wise and pious! But really such a statement exhibits a great deal of naiveté. Why is this naïve? Because people simply can't help themselves, they simply can't be objective—no matter who we are, no matter how smart, unbiased, rational, critical, or right we think we are. We automatically interpret the Bible as *we* read it, through our own grid, our own set of glasses.

Just consider how your own understanding of particular words and phrases may be a shade different from the next person's. When you tell a computer tech that you have a mouse problem and then tell a pest exterminator the same thing, they don't hear you the same, and they certainly don't see it the same in their mind's eye. Likewise, your personal history, knowledge of vocabulary, understanding of Biblical times are uniquely yours.

Take the phrase, "Our Father in heaven." Your personal history may include physical abuse by your father; or perhaps you had a wonderful father; then again, maybe you've had a radical feminist background. There are so many illustrations like this that show us how our personal differences in temperament and experience cause us to interpret not only life but the Scriptures differently from others.

If you suffer with a low self-esteem and feel inferior and deserving of punishment, you may read the Scriptures and see God and the Christian life primarily in categories of fear, dread, judgment, and hell. God may seem unapproachable to you, leading you to doubt your salvation or that God really cares for you.

On the other hand, you may be one who reads the very same Scriptures, but from the perspective of someone who has enjoyed love, peace, and security from early childhood. As a result, you may see God and the Christian life primarily in categories of love, blessing, assurance, and joy.

We are all unique, with our own lenses through which we interpret everything we hear, see, and experience. While God's Word is perfectly true, none of us can always perfectly interpret it. Only Christ, who is sinless and in every way whole, can perfectly perceive reality and God's truths without any flaw in His understanding.

This is one reason why it is so important to participate in the body of Christ—in our local church, but also in the *larger* body of Christ. As we study God's Word together, with the Holy Spirit as our guide, we can usually arrive at a far more balanced and accurate view of the Scriptures than any of us can by ourselves. It is *because of* our differences that we *need* each other. Our own biases get exposed, our blind spots become apparent, our misunderstandings of certain ideas get corrected, and we learn from one another.

I mention all this to make a key point: *Because* we all have inadequacies, biases, blind spots, and misconceptions, we should remain somewhat *humble* about our own points of view. We should be open, teachable, and ready to see an enlarged or clearer truth from God's Word that we will miss if we are too individualistic or dogmatic. I'm not suggesting that we be wishy-washy about the central doctrines of our faith. Nor do I suggest we become less than firm in our commitment to the authority of Scripture. What I *am* saying is that God wants to bring His church into harmony concerning the ministry of the Holy Spirit. For this to come about, we must be *humble* about our own understandings, *open* to His Spirit as He seeks to balance our theological viewpoints, and *eager* to maintain the unity of the Spirit.

Avoiding non-Biblical Presuppositions

One problem we face as we seek to come together in our theology of the Holy Spirit concerns our presuppositions. Sometimes we as individuals or as movements and denominations, acquire doctrinal presuppositions that are not sufficiently substantiated or justified by the Scriptures. This, of course, is a problem in the secular academic world, as well. A secular example is how humanistic teachers and professors present atheistic Darwinian evolution as fact, rather than theory. They hold to unproven and unjustified assumptions, leaving no crack for Intelligent Design, simply because they cannot stand the thought of a Creator God.

It may come as a surprise that Christians also make assumptions that the Scriptures do not substantiate. We can decide, for example, that because God is love, verses that refer to His wrath against sin are incompatible with His love and therefore not quite as authoritative.

Or, we can presuppose that God means for us to take every passage of Scripture literally, that none of it is allegorical or symbolic. So when we come to the book of Revelation and its incredible visions of dragons and multi-headed beasts, we interpret them literally rather than seeing that apocalyptic literature is very much filled with symbols. The symbols point to reality and truths but are not intended to be taken literally themselves.

When we approach the Scriptures, we need to do so with integrity and with openness into new insights into God's truth, even if our own preferred meaning is something else. We are in error if we approach the Scriptures with our minds already made up before we know what the texts actually say. When it comes to certain issues involving the Holy Spirit, some of us may already have our minds made up before even knowing what the Scriptures actually have to say about them. Here are some examples:

- God gives the gift of tongues to every believer who wants it, and every Christian could speak in tongues if he or she so desired.
- God no longer gives us the supernatural gifts like prophecy, tongues, or healing. Those gifts stopped after the apostles died.
- The baptism in the Holy Spirit is a second experience that follows being born again.

These statements are examples of widely held beliefs; but do the Scriptures readily substantiate them? Now I may be pushing some buttons with some of you right now. You may be reacting, "Yes, of course the Scriptures do!" about one or two of them. But it may be helpful to ask yourself, "Is my strongly held conviction about these things valid? Is it derived more from a commitment to a particular theological position than from the Scriptures themselves?" To have true integrity, we must carefully avoid temptations to judge the Scriptures by our theological convictions rather than letting the Scriptures judge our theological convictions. *That is, we should allow Scripture to shape our theology rather than allow our theology to force an interpretation of Scripture that Scripture does not justify.*

More About Interpretation

Evangelical Christians treasure the right of individuals, aided by the Holy Spirit, to interpret the Scriptures for themselves. But many pitfalls exist, and we must be careful to avoid them as we exercise this freedom. Paul the apostle urged Timothy, "Do your best to present yourself to God as one approved, a workman who does not need to be ashamed and who correctly handles the word of truth," (2 Timothy 2:15). We must do our best to learn as much as we can about interpreting the Scriptures responsibly and correctly.

We Christians make numerous mistakes in this area of interpretation, and I am sure I still have blind spots in my thinking, too. I look back in real embarrassment at some of the things I once believed and taught earlier in my Christian life and ministry. I remember when, as a new convert, I chose to read the book of Leviticus. As I started wading through the dietary and sanitary laws and read about the penalties for various offenses, I wondered what on earth I had gotten myself into. "Oh, no," I remember thinking to myself, "I've got to stop eating ham and bacon and oysters and shrimp!" It wasn't until later that I learned an important principle of interpreting the Scriptures: Because Christ *fulfills* the Old Testament, we must always interpret the Old Testament from a New Testament perspective.

Later, I came to see that Christ declared all foods "clean," and that what goes into a person isn't what defiles, but what comes out of his heart (see Matthew 15:10–20). Christ fulfilled the ceremonial laws, Sabbath laws, and feast days which Scripture says were mere shadows of the *reality* to come. The *Reality* is Jesus Christ and a personal relationship with Him (see Colossians 2:16ff).

We Christians face a number of other problems when we interpret the Scriptures. Because of them we end up with widely divergent views on doctrinal issues. Some of these views are erroneous and even dangerous. The following are typical of these problems:

1. We may take what God speaks to our hearts *devotionally* and then expand the devotional thought or inspiration to doctrine. At times God's Spirit may use particular verses or passages of Scripture completely out of their context to speak to us about personal needs for hope, healing, guidance, and so forth. However, when seeking doctrinal truth, it isn't appropriate to use passages of Scripture without regard for their historical or literary context. Many so-called "new revelations" are born this way, and sometimes, sectarian views and even heretical cults emerge from this misuse of scripture.

2. We Christians sometimes interpret the Bible by our own spiritual experiences and tend to extend or absolutize what we experience into a norm that everyone should experience just as we have. We should not, however, interpret the Bible by our experiences, but rather, we must interpret our spiritual experiences (or lack thereof) by the Scriptures. For example: One Christian prays for and receives a spiritual filling but does *not* receive a prayer language. This person concludes that tongues cannot be for today. Another Christian prays and receives a prayer language, concluding that everyone should speak in tongues. We must realize that the Holy Spirit—like the wind—moves differently in different lives. Our own experiences may not match what God desires to do in everyone else. Unless my experiences are clearly presented as norms in the Scriptures, I am presumptuous to believe *my* experiences should be the norm for everyone else.

3. We often *proof-text,* that is, we seek to prove a doctrinal point by quoting or referring to a Scripture that, when understood in its historical and literary contexts,[27] has nothing to do with the point we are trying to prove. For example: I have known Christians who seek to prove the validity of a "positive confession" teaching by using Job 3:25 where Job says, "What I feared has come upon me." They say that this verse *proves* that, because Job confessed negatively, all his woes came upon him. They use this verse out of its literary context when it really has *nothing* to do with Job's woes. Reading chapter l, we get the true picture. God allowed Satan to test Job's loyalty and faith. This is not to say that a positive confession of faith or positive outlook on life is unimportant. It does illustrate, however, how the Bible gets mishandled.

4. We sometimes base a doctrine or viewpoint on a particular passage or two, neglecting the other passages pertinent to correctly understanding God's truth. For example, we may base our understanding of the doctrine of eternal security on Romans 8:37–39, that nothing "will be able to separate us from the love of God . . ." But then we might ignore passages like Galatians 5:2l, which denounce those who continue to embrace sinful lifestyles. "I warn you as I did before," Paul wrote, "that those who live like this will not inherit the Kingdom of God." It is vitally important that we be committed to *BALANCE*, and that we take *ALL* relevant

---

[27] The "historical context" of a passage of Scripture is the "Who? What? When? Why? Where? What's the point?" questions that give us a feel for what God was saying to the original hearers, why He was saying it, and so forth. We try to find out as much as we can about what was happening culturally, spiritually, economically, politically, etc. so that our understanding of God's Word will be as clear as possible. The "Literary context" refers to the placement of a passage of Scripture among other passages. We best understand a verse or passage—as we would a personal letter to ourselves—when we read it in the context of surrounding passages.

Scriptures into account and not just those that support our preferred viewpoint or understanding.

5. Sometimes we make a doctrinal norm from a *description* or *narrative* when the Scriptures do not justify it. One example is the practice of releasing rattlesnakes in church because of the Mark 16:17–18, passage where Jesus said, "And these signs will accompany those who believe: In My name they will . . . pick up snakes with their hands; and when they drink deadly poison, it will not hurt them at all . . . ." We know that the apostle Paul lived after being bitten by a poisonous snake. Obviously, this illustrates the kinds of things Jesus said would happen as we walk in faith. But does that justify our interpreting Jesus' words as a command to release snakes in church? I think not!

   Here's another example: We deduce that every Christian should, can, and will speak in tongues based upon the *description* of what took place at Pentecost in Acts 2:4, "All of them were filled with the Holy Spirit and began to speak in other tongues . . . ." However, it is inappropriate to use descriptions or narratives as the only basis for doctrinal norms or commands. Descriptions can be used to *illustrate* doctrinal norms that are clearly taught as such elsewhere in the Scriptures; however, descriptions alone cannot be used to *establish* doctrinal norms.

6. Related to Number 5 is the practice of teaching a required pattern of God's working based on a description or narrative. For example, one believes that the baptism of the Spirit is a *second* experience, subsequent to conversion, based on the description of the life of Jesus who was conceived by the Spirit at birth and later baptized by the Spirit after His water

baptism. The description of Jesus Christ's unique experience as God's Son is not sufficient by itself to establish a doctrine as to how the Holy Spirit will work in the lives of believers. To justify this belief as a doctrinal norm, the Scriptures must clearly teach this pattern for believers elsewhere. Again, we should consider *all* pertinent passages of Scripture—not just those that support our preferred viewpoint.

7. We often fail to differentiate between what is *normal* and what is *normative*. To say that an experience is *normal* is to say that it is typical, usual, commonly experienced. Normal biblical experiences would include regeneration, being filled with the Spirit, speaking in tongues, healing, miracles. We find all these experiences in the Bible. They happen. On the other hand, to say that an experience is *normative* is to say, "These things happen, and they must happen this way, by this pattern, for everybody, all the time."

   Biblically supported spiritual experiences that are both normal and normative include: The experience of salvation by grace through faith; and, the experience of being born-again to enter the kingdom of God. Salvation by grace through faith is commonly experienced (*normal*) and it *must* be experienced in order to be a Christian (*normative*). To say that a second experience in the Spirit is *normal* is to say that such second experiences are biblically supportable and desirable, as breakthroughs, renewal, and growth experiences but that they do not necessarily fit a particular pattern, nor are they necessarily experienced by all Christians the same way. To say that a second experience is *normative* is to say that it is a necessary experience for every believer and must happen in a prescribed pattern or with prescribed results. We need to be careful not to take experiences that are *normal,* e.g., "these things happen," and make them *normative*, e.g., "they must happen in this way for every Christian," *unless* Scripture warrants this. I believe mistakes in this area cause many unnecessary divisions in our understanding of the Holy Spirit's workings.

8. When we interpret the Bible, many of us have not learned to apply the *"Explicit, Implicit, Speculation Test." Explicit* refers to those doctrines or teachings that the Scriptures substantiate clearly and specifically, such as the atoning death of Christ and the power of His blood to effect the forgiveness of sins. Numerous Scriptures make this clear, for example, Ephesians 1:7, "In Him we have redemption through His blood, the forgiveness of sins." Another example: Christ rose from the dead, a fact stated explicitly and repeatedly in the New Testament.

   Implicit refers to those doctrines or teachings that are clearly substantiated in the Scriptures, but not explicitly. One example is the doctrine of the Trinity (One God exists in three Persons: Father, Son, and Holy Spirit), based on such passages as Ephesians 2:18 ("For through *Him* [Christ], we both have access to the *Father* by *one Spirit*"), and 2 Corinthians 13:14 ("May the grace of the Lord *Jesus Christ*, and the love of *God*, and the fellowship of the *Holy Spirit* be with you all.") These, along with many other passages, support the personality and deity of all three members of the Triune God—Father, Son, and Holy Spirit.

   Speculation refers to doctrinal beliefs based on interpretations of passages of Scripture that are neither explicitly nor implicitly applicable and thus are guesses or speculations. One example of this is when we use 2 Thessalonians 2:6–7 to substantiate the belief in a pre-tribulation rapture (the belief that Christ will take His people out of the world *before* the seven-year tribulation period that precedes His second coming). I'm not trying to debate eschatological issues here, just issues of interpretation. If we look at this passage, we see that it refers to a Restrainer that holds back the man of lawlessness until such time as the Restrainer is removed and the man of lawlessness is revealed. The Scriptures do not identify who or what the Restrainer is. Theories of the Restrainer's identity include government, the Holy Spirit, and the archangel Michael, among others. Because the Scriptures are neither explicit nor implicit with regard to the Restrainer's identity, we are left only to *speculate.* Some commentators speculate that the Restrainer is the Holy Spirit. Based upon that speculation, they further speculate that, if the Holy Spirit is taken out of the way, it must mean He entirely leaves the world. Then, a third speculation based on the two preceding ones forms: Since the Holy Spirit is taken out of the world, then all Christians (the church) in whom the Holy Spirit dwells must also be taken out of the world. Finally, what doctrine do we have? The Pre-Trib Rapture? Not good!

I hope it is clear to you that, whatever may be your views on the Rapture of the church, *speculative* interpretations of Scripture to support doctrine are not helpful; in fact, they are generally inadequate and often lead to erroneous conclusions. Doctrines can be established only on the basis of explicit and implicit biblical passages, not on speculation. It is all right to speculate when the Scriptures are unclear, but only if we acknowledge that we are speculating, and only when no doctrinal weight is put on our speculations.

As we seek to come to a balanced and accurate understanding of the Holy Spirit and His ministries in, among, and through God's people, we must apply these (and other) principles of interpretation.

APPENDIX B

Finding Freedom from Handles of the Enemy

When we accept Christ as our Lord and Savior, He forgives our past sins. Sometimes, however, there are "handles" that the enemy has in our lives as a result of those past sins. He can use those handles to hinder and defeat us and prevent us from being filled with the Holy Spirit. Satan gets these handles through several key areas in our lives. We need to identify them so we can experience the victory Christ has already made possible for us through His cross and resurrection.

One of those areas is *the occult.* Have you ever involved yourself in any form of spiritual experiences other than that of biblical Christianity? If so, you opened the door for a spirit or spirits other than the Holy Spirit to influence your life. Following the steps of James 5:16 can enable us to break these occult handles. Confess your involvement and repent of it forcefully as an act of your will. Say something like this:

> I confess that I have sinned by _____________ (whatever the sin is). Thank you, Lord, that you forgive me and cleanse me by the blood of Jesus Christ. I renounce (this sin) in Jesus' name. I renounce Satan and any demonic handle that has attached itself to this past sin in my life — in Jesus' name. I ask you now, Lord Jesus, to fill me afresh with your Holy Spirit. Amen.

Recently I prayed with a committed Christian woman, and a leader, who said she always got very sleepy when the Holy Spirit was moving in a powerful way, whether in a personal quiet time or in a worship service. I asked her if she had ever been involved in any non-Christian religious experiences. She thought about it, and then she told me she had been to a Zen Buddhist retreat and also had attended a Dalai Lama event. I said, "That would do it!" I led her through the confession and prayers, and then I prayed for her. She was immediately set free, and I heard from her later that she stayed up reading her Bible that night until 2am, wide awake and very excited in God's powerful presence!

Another key area where Satan gets handles in our lives is *unforgiveness and bitterness*. We have all been wronged or hurt by others. For that reason, most of us have to fight against the human tendency to be bitter and unforgiving. When we pray the Lord's Prayer, we become acquainted with the fact that experiencing God's forgiveness for our sins is significantly linked with *our* willingness to forgive others for their sins against us. Jesus said it clearly:

> If you forgive those who sin against you, your heavenly Father will forgive you. But if you refuse to forgive others, your Father will not forgive your sins. (Matthew 6:14–15, NLT)

Before you can be filled with the Holy Spirit, you must forgive those whom you have need to forgive. Sometimes we have repressed bitterness and unforgiveness towards some person or group, and we may not even be aware of it. But rest assured, bitterness and unforgiveness—whether repressed or conscious—adversely affects our spiritual lives.

Ask the Holy Spirit to remind you of any and every person you need to forgive. Repent of harboring bitterness, and renounce it in Jesus' name. Then forgive the person(s) as an act of your will. You may not *feel* like forgiving, but your will is more important than your emotions. Emotional healing can come only as we let go of bitterness and let the Spirit of God minister in His love and power to our souls. You may need to pray through this area with one or two other Christian friends; if your bitterness has become deeply entrenched, you will need their encouraging support and prayers and also their help in keeping you free.

It is important when you forgive to say, "*I forgive . . .*" not "I *want* to forgive" or "God, help me forgive." We obey God when we actually forgive, not when we merely express our desire to forgive or ask for His help to do so.

A third key area where Satan gets handles in our lives relates to *habitual sins*. Often habitual sins become addictions or obsessions. "Like a city whose walls are broken down is a man who lacks self-control" (Proverbs 25:28). Experiencing sinful sexual pleasure, for example, can quickly become an addiction, whether the sin is homosexual or heterosexual. I have found in ministering to people that they often have a "one-flesh" bondage that must be broken by a verbal repentance and renunciation of the sin. For example, "I repent of the sin of sexual immorality with (that person) and I renounce the sinful one-flesh bondage in the name of Jesus Christ." This verbal renunciation may not be necessary in every instance, but I am convinced that at times it is.

Cheri and I were once ministering to a woman in her late twenties whom we had known for a while. She had been a Christian for about a year when we first met her. One night as we prayed with her, she began convulsing, and I got a mental picture of a man, so I asked her about him. We had previously learned that she had lived with a warlock for seven years and that she had been a prostitute during that period to support a heroin addiction. When I told her about the mental picture I saw, she acknowledged a spiritual bondage to the man. We led her to renounce the sinful one-flesh bondage and all demonic handles that had resulted from it. After she forcefully renounced them twice, she stopped convulsing. We asked her if she had kept letters or gifts from their past relationship. She acknowledged she had, and she brought us a bag full of pictures, letters and trinkets that had helped hold her in bondage. That night she threw those things away. She was *free!* A short time later God brought a Christian man into her life. They were soon a very happily married Christian couple.

Here, in summary, are some steps to take in order to experience freedom in Christ: First, confess your sin to one or two trusted and mature Christians. Second, firmly and verbally (aloud) renounce, in Jesus' name, the sin and any demonic "handle" attached to that sin in your life. Third, ask your friends to pray for your forgiveness, cleansing, victory, and for a fresh infilling of the Holy Spirit. Then thank God and praise Him for His forgiveness, cleansing, and restoration in your life.

Spiritual Journey Press Order Form

To order additional copies of **Called to High Adventure** or other Spiritual Journey Press books, please complete this order form and mail it to: Spiritual Journey Press, P.O. Box 3041, Mercerville, New Jersey 08619. Also, you may wish to visit the Spiritual Journey Press web site: www.spiritualjourneypress.com. All of our books also may be ordered through Amazon.com.

Please ship my order to:

Name: ____

Address: ____

City, State, Zip Code: ________________________________

E-Mail (for confirmation): ____________________________

I would like to order:

_____ copies of **Called to High Adventure** @ $14.95 each $ _________

_____ copies of **Endless Possibilities** @ $11.95 each $ _________

_____ copies of the **EP Course Book** @ $13.95 each $ _________

_____ copies of **A Summer's Journey** @ $14.95 each $ _________

_____ copies of **Journeying with Joshua** @ $14.95 each $ _________

_____ copies of **Jesus Christ from Cover to Cover** @ $19.95 each $ _________

Postage and handling ($1.00 per book): $ _________

New Jersey residents add 7.0% sales tax: $ _________

TOTAL AMOUNT ENCLOSED: $ ___________

MAKE CHECKS PAYABLE TO: Spiritual Journey Press